WORKBOOK
Accounting Fundamentals

SIXTH EDITION

Michael G. Curran, Jr., Ed.D.
Associate Professor
Rider University
Lawrenceville, New Jersey

Esther D. Flashner, A.B., M.S., C.P.A.
Former Associate Professor of Accounting
Hunter College of the City University of New York
New York, New York

New York, New York   Columbus, Ohio   Woodland Hills, California   Peoria, Illinois

Glencoe/McGraw-Hill 
A Division of The ***McGraw-Hill*** *Companies*

Send all inquiries to:
Glencoe/McGraw-Hill
21600 Oxnard Street, Suite 500
Woodland Hills, CA 91367-4906

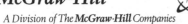

P/N G27518.59
Part of ISBN 0-07-822748-8
0-07-822749-6 (Computerized version)

Printed in the United States of America.

3 4 5 6 7 8 9 047 05 04 03

CONTENTS

Chapter 1

PRINCIPLES OF ACCOUNTING

Name ______________________

Date ______________________

Exercise 1-1

1.	______________	6.	______________
2.	______________	7.	______________
3.	______________	8.	______________
4.	______________	9.	______________
5.	______________	10.	______________

Exercise 1-2

	Assets	=	Liabilities	+	Owner's Equity
1.	$18,000	=	$13,000	+	________
2.	$10,000	=	________	+	$3,000
3.	________	=	$7,000	+	$8,000
4.	$25,000	=	________	+	$15,000
5.	$40,000	=	$10,000	+	________
6.	________	=	$20,000	+	$25,000

Exercise 1-3

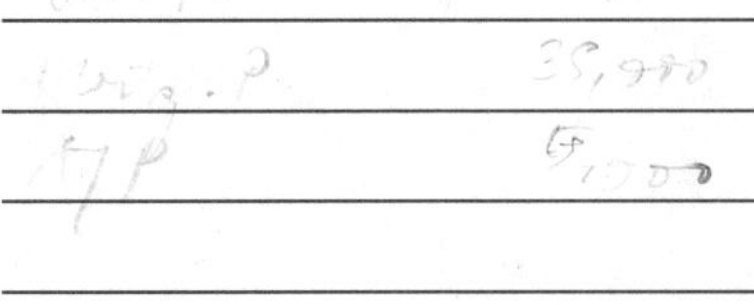

Assets		Liabilities		Owner's Equity	
________	____	________	____	________	____
________	____	________	____	________	____
________	____	________	____	________	____
________	____	________	____	________	____
________	____	________	____	________	____
________	____	________	____	________	____
Total	____	Total	____	Total	____

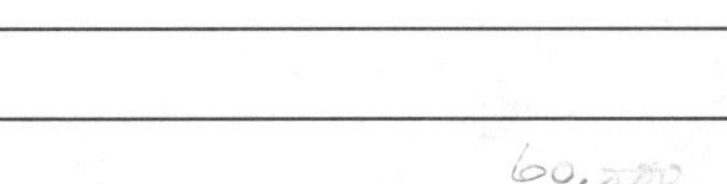

Total Assets ____________ = Total Liabilities and Owner's Equity ____________

Exercise 1-4

	Balance Sheet Item Affected	Increase or Decrease
1.		
2.		
3.		
4.		
5.		
6.		
7.		
8.		
9.		
10.		

Problem 1-1

Name ____________________

Assets					=	Liabilities	+	Owner's Equity
Cash	+		+		=		+	
$8,000	+	$	+	$	=	$	+	$
Totals		$			=		$	

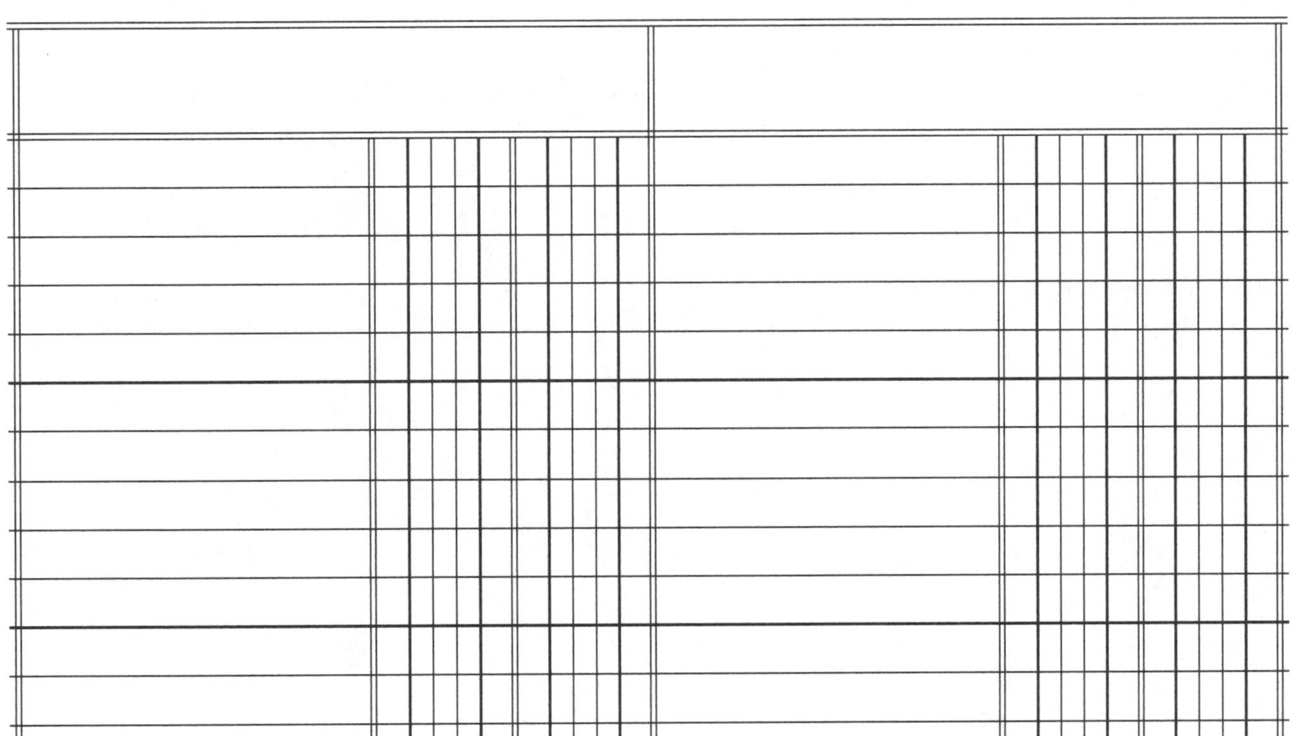

See the self-check key at the back of this workbook.

Problem 1-2

	Balance Sheet Items Affected	Increased or Decreased	Amount
a. 1.	Cash	Increased	$ 1,500
2.	Patricia Brennan, Capital	Increased	1,500
b. 1.			
2.			
c. 1.			
2.			
d. 1.			
2.			
e. 1.			
2.			
f. 1.			
2.			
g. 1.			
2.			

See the self-check key at the back of this workbook.

Problem 1-3

Name ______________________

	Assets					=	Liabilities	+	Owner's Equity
	Cash	+	Office Equipment	+	Landscaping Equipment	=	Accounts Payable	+	Duke Brady, Capital
Totals	$6,000	+	$4,000	+	$20,000	=	$5,000	+	$25,000
Transaction a									
New Totals									
Transaction b									
New Totals									
Transaction c									
New Totals									
Transaction d									
New Totals									
Transaction e									
New Totals									

Assets: $____________

____

____

Total $____________

Assets $____________ = Liabilities $____________ + Owner's Equity $____________

See the self-check key at the back of this workbook.

Problem 1-4

	Assets					=	Liabilities	+	Owner's Equity
	Cash	+	Supplies	+	Office Equipment	=	Accounts Payable	+	Ronald Gant, Capital
Totals	$5,500	+	$100	+	$3,400	=	$1,600	+	$7,400
Transaction a									
New Totals									
Transaction b									
New Totals									
Transaction c									
New Totals									
Transaction d									
New Totals									
Transaction e									
New Totals									
Transaction f									
New Totals									

Assets: $__________

____

____

Total $__________

Assets $__________ = Liabilities $__________ + Owner's Equity $__________

See the self-check key at the back of this workbook.

Case Study 1

Name ______________________________

Extra Form

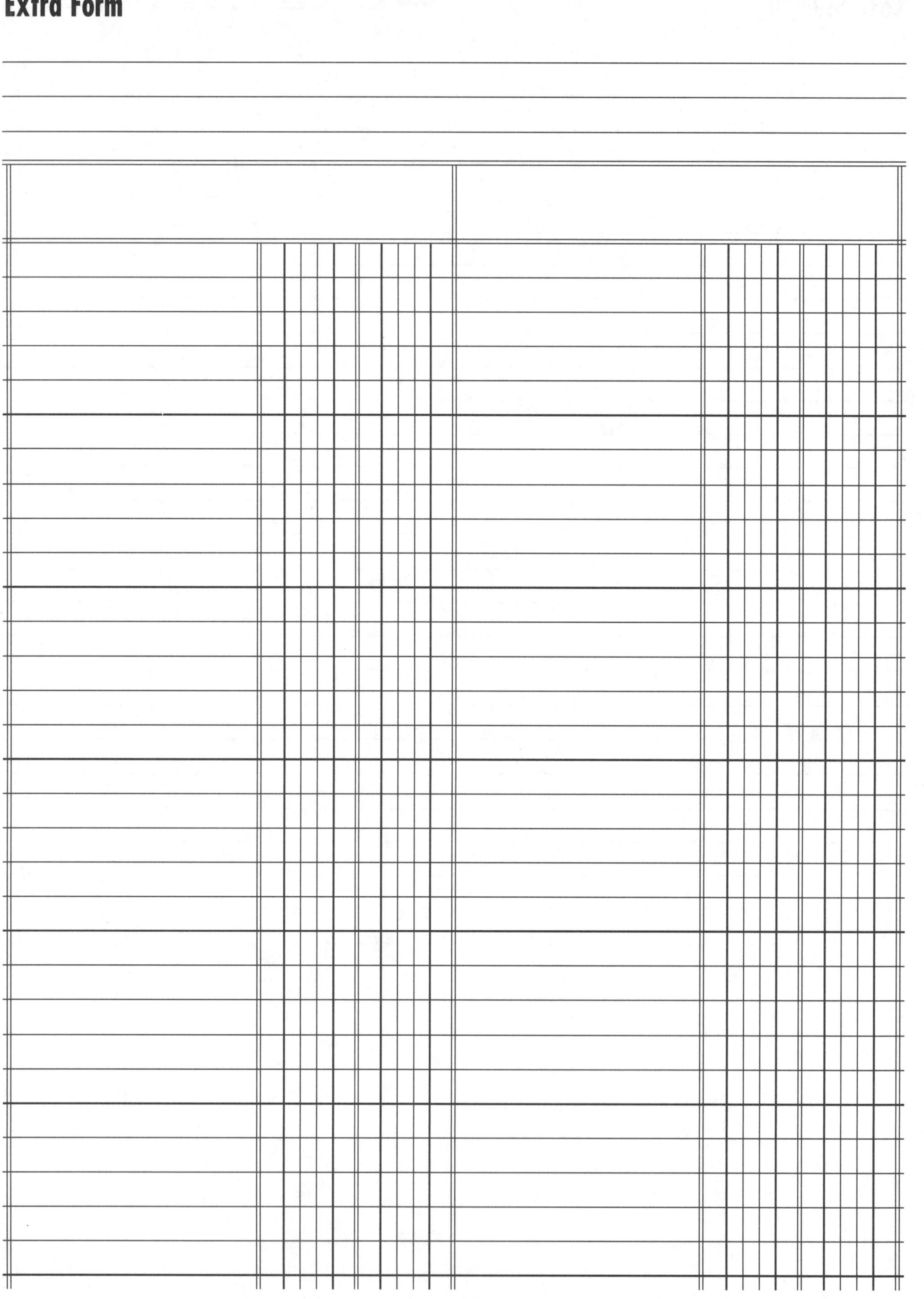

Chapter 2

Name ______________________________

Date ______________________________

THE EFFECT OF REVENUE AND EXPENSES

Exercise 2-1

Instruction 1

Total Revenue __________ – Total Expenses __________ = Net Income __________

Instruction 2

Elmer Mears, Capital, June 1, 20xx $__________
Add Net Income __________
Elmer Mears, Capital, June 30, 20xx __________

Instruction 3

Assets $__________ = Liabilities $__________ + Owner's Equity $__________

Exercise 2-2

Instruction 1

Total Revenue __________ – Total Expenses __________ = Net Loss __________

Instruction 2

Juan Diaz, Capital, May 1, 20xx $__________
Deduct Net Loss __________
Juan Diaz, Capital, May 31, 20xx $__________

Instruction 3

Assets $__________ = Liabilities $__________ + Owner's Equity $__________

Exercise 2-3

Example: Cash invested by owner.

	+Assets	+Owner's Equity
1.		
2.		
3.		
4.		
5.		
6.		
7.		
8.		
9.		
10.		

Exercise 2-4

Problem 2-1

Name ______________________________

Instruction 1

	Assets					=	Liabilities	+	Owner's Equity			
	Cash	+	Accounts Receivable	+	Equipment	=	Accounts Payable	+	Lisa Valdez, Capital	+	Revenue	–	Expenses
	$8,000	+	$3,000	+	$7,000	=	$4,000	+	$14,000	+	$ 0	–	$ 0
Transaction a													
Totals													
Transaction b													
Totals													
Transaction c													
Totals													
Transaction d													
Totals													
Transaction e													
Totals													
Transaction f													
Totals													
Transaction g													
Totals													

Instruction 2

Revenue	$________	Lisa Valdez, Capital, July 1	$________
Less Expenses	________	Add Net Income or Deduct Net Loss	________
Net Income (Loss)	$________	Lisa Valdez, Capital, July 31	$________

Instruction 3

Assets $__________ = Liabilities $__________ + Owner's Equity $__________

See the self-check key at the back of this workbook.

Problem 2-2

Instruction 1

	Assets					=	Liabilities	+	Owner's Equity				
	Cash	+	Accounts Receivable	+	Equipment	=	Accounts Payable	+	Dale Neeld, Capital	+	Revenue	−	Expenses
Transaction a													
Totals													
Transaction b													
Totals													
Transaction c													
Totals													
Transaction d													
Totals													
Transaction e													
Totals													
Transaction f													
Totals													
Transaction g													
Totals													
Transaction h													
Totals													
Transaction i													
Totals													

Instruction 2

Revenue	$	Dale Neeld, Capital, June 5	$
Less Expenses		Add Net Income or Deduct Net Loss	
Net Income (Loss)	$	Dale Neeld, Capital, June 30	$

Instruction 3

Assets $________ = Liabilities $________ + Owner's Equity $________

See the self-check key at the back of this workbook.

Problem 2-3

Name ____________________

Instruction 1

	Assets			=	Liabilities	+	Owner's Equity		
	Cash	+ Accounts Receivable	+ Equipment	=	Accounts Payable	+	Brenda Burg, Capital	+ Revenue	− Expenses
Transaction a									
Totals									
Transaction b									
Totals									
Transaction c									
Totals									
Transaction d									
Totals									
Transaction e									
Totals									
Transaction f									
Totals									
Transaction g									
Totals									
Transaction h									
Totals									
Transaction i									
Totals									
Transaction j									
Totals									

Instructions 2 and 3

Revenue	$	Brenda Burg, Capital, May 1	$
Less Expenses		Add Net Income or Deduct Net Loss	
Net Income (Loss)	$	Brenda Burg, Capital, May 31	$

Instruction 4

Assets $__________ = Liabilities $__________ + Owner's Equity $__________

See the self-check key at the back of this workbook.

Problem 2-4

Revenue		
Commissions		$
Expenses		
Rent Expense	$	
Salaries Expense		
Advertising Expense		
Telephone Expense		
Postage Expense		
Total Expenses		
Net Income (Loss)		$

See the self-check key at the back of this workbook.

Case Study 2

Name ______________________________

Extra Form

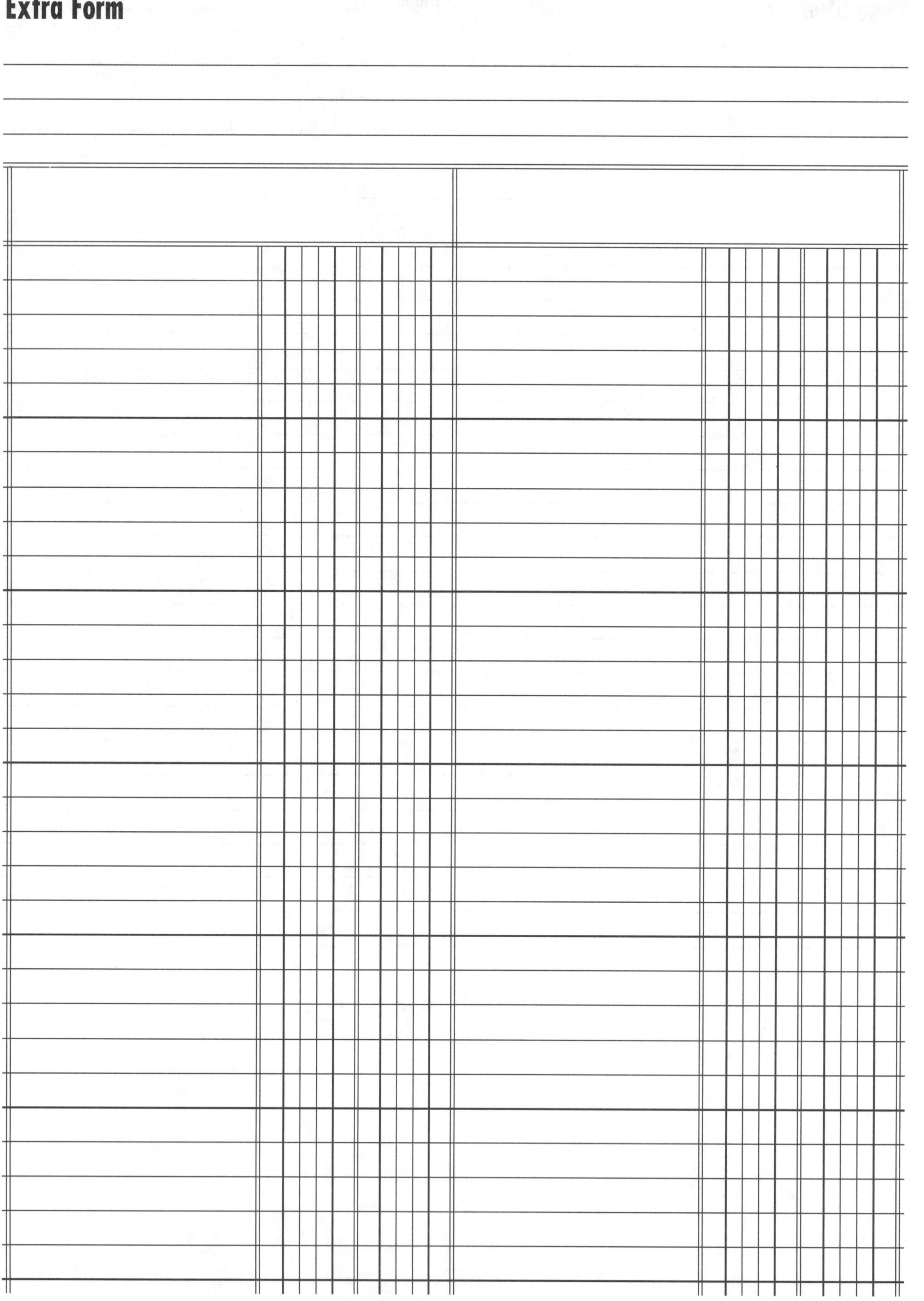

Chapter 3

Name ______________________________

Date______________________________

ASSET, LIABILITY, AND OWNER'S EQUITY ACCOUNTS

Exercise 3-1

a. ______________________________

b. ______________________________

c. ______________________________

d. ______________________________

e. ______________________________

Exercise 3-2

Cash

(Ex.)	20,000	(a)	400
(c)	400	(d)	500
(e)	5,000		

Equipment

(a)	400	(c)	400
(b)	1,000		

Accounts Payable

(d)	500	(b)	1,000

Susie Simmons, Capital

		(Ex.)	20,000
		(e)	5,000

Assets $____________ = Liabilities $____________ + Owner's Equity $____________

Exercise 3-3

Assets $____________ = Liabilities $____________ + Owner's Equity $____________

Exercise 3-4

Assets $____________ = Liabilities $____________ + Owner's Equity $____________

See the self-check key at the back of this workbook.

Problem 3-1

Name ______________________________

Assets: $ ____________

____

____

____

____

Total $ ____________

Assets $ ____________ = Liabilities $ ____________ + Owner's Equity $ ____________

See the self-check key at the back of this workbook.

Problem 3-2

Assets: $______

______

______

______

______

Total $______

Assets $______ = Liabilities $______ + Owner's Equity $______

See the self-check key at the back of this workbook.

Case Study 3

Name

Extra Form

Chapter 4

Name ______________________________

Date ______________________________

REVENUE AND EXPENSE ACCOUNTS

Exercise 4-1

a. ______________________________

b. ______________________________

c. ______________________________

d. ______________________________

e. ______________________________

Exercise 4-2

Instruction 1

Cash

(Ex.)	9,000	(b)	400
(a)	600	(d)	500
(e)	800		

Allen Marcus, Capital

		(Ex.)	9,000

Dental Fees

		(a)	600
		(c)	1,400

Accounts Receivable

(c)	1,400	(e)	800

Allen Marcus, Withdrawals

(d)	500		

Salaries Expense

(b)	400		

Instruction 2

Revenue

_______________ $_______

Operating Expenses

_______________ _______

Net Income $_______

Instruction 3

Owner's Equity

_______________________ _______

_______________________ _______

_______________________ _______

_______________________ _______

_______________________ _______

Instruction 4

Assets = Liabilities + Owner's Equity

_______ = _______ + _______

Exercise 4-3

Name ______________________

Instruction 1

<u>Revenue</u>

Consultation Fees		________
<u>Operating Expenses</u>		
Rent Expense	________	
Salaries Expense	________	
Telephone Expense	________	
Professional Expense	________	
Office Expense	________	
Total Operating Expenses		________
<u>Net Loss</u>		________
<u>Owner's Equity</u>		
Gerald White, Capital		________
Net Loss	________	
Withdrawals	________	
Net Decrease in Owner's Equity		________
Gerald White, Capital		________

Instruction 2

Assets	=	Liabilities	+	Owner's Equity
________	=	________	+	________

Exercise 4-4

Instructions 1-4

Instruction 5

<u>Revenue</u>

Legal Fees

<u>Operating Expenses</u>

Rent Expense

Telephone Expense

Professional Expenses

Total Operating Expenses

<u>Net Income</u>

Instruction 6

<u>Owner's Equity</u>

Sandy Hoffman, Capital

Net Income

Withdrawals

Net Increase in Owner's Equity

Sandy Hoffman, Capital

Instruction 7

Assets	=	Liabilities	+	Owner's Equity
	=		+	

Problem 4-1

Name ____________________

Cash	
14,000	

Accounts Payable	
	7,000

Accounting Fees	

Joseph Barbagallo, Capital	
	32,000

Salaries Expense	

Accounts Receivable	

Joseph Barbagallo, Withdrawals	

Rent Expense	

Office Equipment	
12,000	

Automobile Expense	

Automobile	
13,000	

Note: Save the accounts for use in Problem 5-2.

Problem 4-1 (continued)

Revenue		
Accounting Fees		$
Expenses		
Salaries Expense	$	
Rent Expense		
Automobile Expense		
Total Expenses		
Net Income (Loss)		$

See the self-check key at the back of this workbook.

Problem 4-2

Name ______________________________

Cash	
24,000	

Accounts Payable	
	11,500

Advertising Fees	

Rita Nichols, Capital	
	38,200

Fashion Show Fees	

Accounts Receivable	
11,000	

Rita Nichols, Withdrawals	

Salaries Expense	

Supplies	
500	

Rent Expense	

Equipment	
12,000	

Office Expense	

Computer Software	
2,200	

Note: Save the accounts for use in Problem 5-3.

Problem 4-2 (continued)

Revenue		
Advertising Fees	$	
Fashion Show Fees		
Total Revenue		$
Expenses		
Salaries Expense	$	
Rent Expense		
Office Expense		
Total Expenses		
Net Income (Loss)		$

See the self-check key at the back of this workbook.

Case Study 4

Name ______________________________

Extra Form

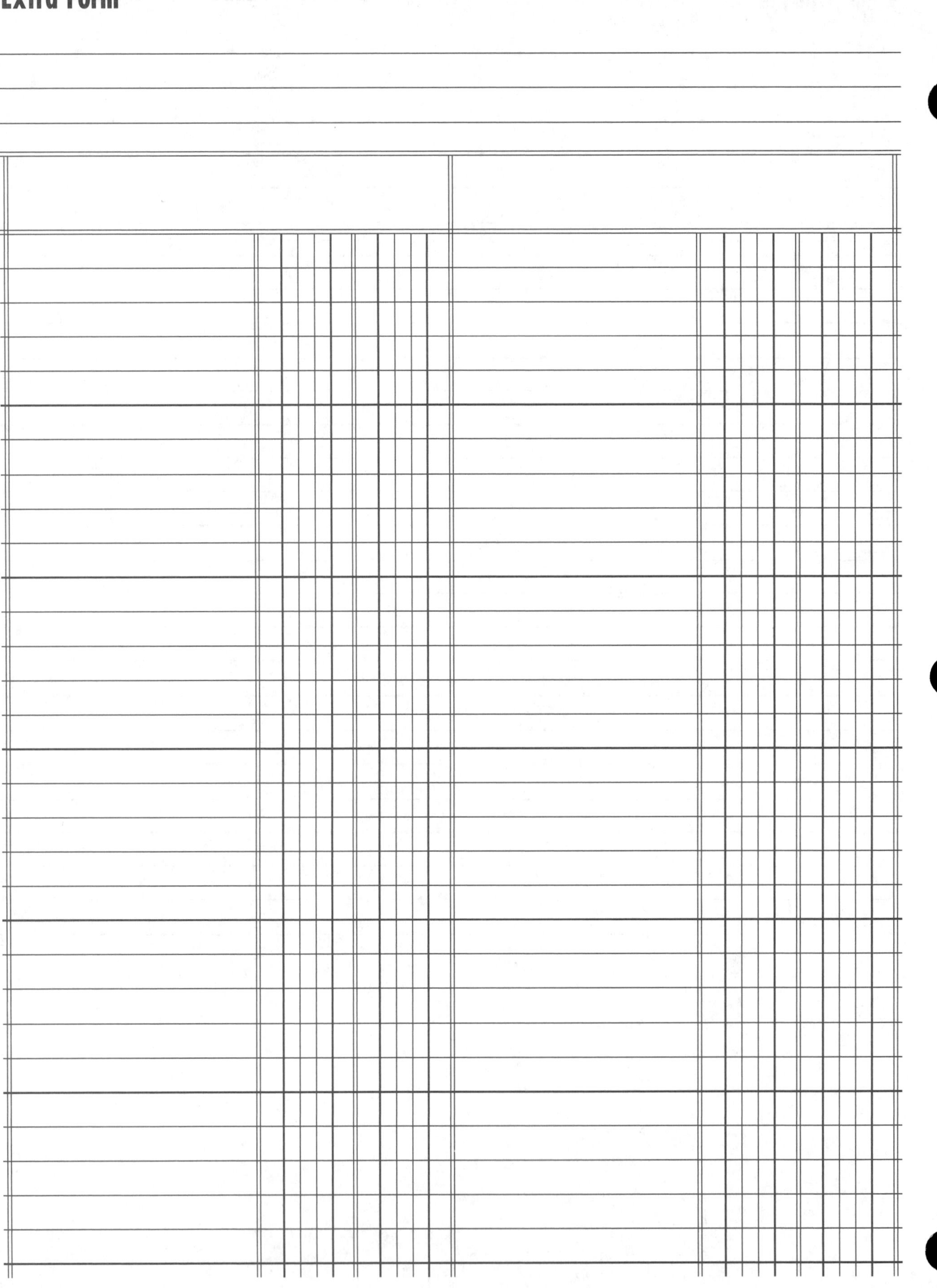

Chapter 5

Name ______________________

Date ______________________

THE TRIAL BALANCE

Exercise 5-1

ACCT. NO.	ACCOUNT NAME	DEBIT	CREDIT

Exercise 5-2

ACCT. NO.	ACCOUNT NAME	DEBIT	CREDIT

Problem 5-1

Cash

	Debit		Credit
	6,000	(b)	225
(a)	2,200	(c)	3,100
(h)	120	(e)	15
(k)	1,200	(g)	110
(n)	1,500	(i)	122
		(j)	20
		(l)	78
		(m)	225

Accounts Receivable

	Debit		Credit
(d)	5,700	(n)	1,500

Office Equipment

	Debit		Credit
	8,300		
(f)	1,980		

Automobile

	Debit		Credit
	12,500		

Building

	Debit		Credit
	79,000		

Accounts Payable

	Debit		Credit
(c)	3,100		4,200
		(f)	1,980

Jim Byelich, Capital

	Debit		Credit
			101,600

Jim Byelich, Withdrawals

	Debit		Credit
(m)	225		

Commissions

	Debit		Credit
		(a)	2,200
		(d)	5,700
		(h)	120
		(k)	1,200

Advertising Expense

	Debit		Credit
(b)	225		
(g)	110		

Automobile Expense

	Debit		Credit
(e)	15		
(j)	20		
(l)	78		

Utilities Expense

	Debit		Credit
(i)	122		

ACCT. NO.	ACCOUNT NAME	DEBIT	CREDIT

See the self-check key at the back of this workbook.

Problem 5-2

Name ______________________

ACCT. NO.	ACCOUNT NAME	DEBIT	CREDIT

See the self-check key at the back of this workbook.

Problem 5-3

ACCT. NO.	ACCOUNT NAME	DEBIT	CREDIT

See the self-check key at the back of this workbook.
Note: Save the trial balance for Problem 6-2.

Problem 5-4

Cash

(a)	26,000	(d)	1,500
(c)	254	(f)	1,200
(e)	568	(g)	800
22,738	26,822	(h)	500
		(i)	84
			4,084

Tim Archibald, Capital

		(a)	62,120

Rent Expense

(d)	1,500		

Equipment

(a)	36,120		
(b)	3,000		
	39,120		

Tim Archibald, Withdrawals

(g)	800		

Salaries Expense

(f)	1,200		

Accounts Payable

(h)	500	(b)	3,000
		2,500	

Cleaning Service Fees

		(c)	254
		(e)	568
			22

Telephone Expense

(i)	84		

ACCT. NO.	ACCOUNT NAME	DEBIT	CREDIT

See the self-check key at the back of this workbook.

Problem 5-5

Name ______________________________

Cash	
	(a) 800
	(b) 700
	(c) 400

John Leidy, Capital	
(c) 400	

Rent Expense	

Equipment	
(b) 700	

John Leidy, Withdrawals	
(a) 800	

ACCT. NO.	ACCOUNT NAME	DEBIT	CREDIT

See the self-check key at the back of this workbook.

Case Study 5

Chapter 6

Name ______________________

Date ______________________

FINANCIAL STATEMENTS

Exercise 6-1

1. ______________________
2. ______________________
3. ______________________
4. ______________________
5. ______________________
6. ______________________
7. ______________________
8. ______________________
9. ______________________

Exercise 6-2

Instruction 1

Revenue

Taxi Fares ______

Operating Expenses

Salaries Expense ______

Repairs Expense ______

Office Expense ______

Total Operating Expenses ______

Net Income ______

Instruction 2

Owner's Equity

Leslie Chan, Capital, June 1, 20XX ______

Additional Investment ______

Total Investment ______

Net Income ______

Less Withdrawals ______

Net Increase in Owner's Equity ______

Leslie Chan, Capital, June 30, 20XX ______

Instruction 3

Assets	=	Liabilities	+	Owner's Equity
______	=	______	+	______

Exercise 6-3

Instruction 1

Revenue

Management Fees		______
Operating Expenses		
Salaries Expense	______	
Rent Expense	______	
Telephone Expense	______	
Advertising Expense	______	
Total Operating Expenses		______
Net Loss		______

Instruction 2

Owner's Equity

Connie Botzer, Capital, December 1, 20XX		______
Additional Investment		______
Total Investment		______
Net Loss	______	
Withdrawals	______	
Net Decrease in Owner's Equity		______
Connie Botzer, Capital, December 31, 20XX		______

Instruction 3

Assets	=	Liabilities	+	Owner's Equity
______	=	______	+	______

Problem 6-1

Name ______________________

Quality Photo Studio

Trial Balance

January 31, 20XX

ACCT. NO.	ACCOUNT NAME	DEBIT	CREDIT
	Cash	11,320.00	
	Accounts Receivable	2,142.00	
	Photographic Equipment	12,900.00	
	Office Equipment	5,750.00	
	Accounts Payable		9,600.00
	Kathleen Bonita, Capital		21,760.00
	Kathleen Bonita, Withdrawals	1,000.00	
	Photographic Service Fees		5,672.00
	Rent Expense	1,160.00	
	Salaries Expense	2,140.00	
	Postage Expense	80.00	
	Advertising Expense	430.00	
	Telephone Expense	110.00	
	Totals	37,032.00	37,032.00

See the self-check key at the back of this workbook.

Problem 6-1 (continued)

See the self-check key at the back of this workbook.

See the self-check key at the back of this workbook.

Problem 6-2

Name ______________________

See the self-check key at the back of this workbook.

See the self-check key at the back of this workbook.

Problem 6-2 (continued)

See the self-check key at the back of this workbook.

Case Study 6

Name ______________________

PROJECT 1

Date ______________________

Cash

Accounts Payable

Advertising Expense

Daniel Van Lieu, Capital

Automobile Expense

Accounts Receivable

Daniel Van Lieu, Withdrawals

Rent Expense

Decorating Service Fees

Office Equipment

Postage Expense

Telephone Expense

Automobile

Project 1 (continued)

ACCT. NO.	ACCOUNT NAME	DEBIT	CREDIT

See the self-check key at the back of this workbook.

See the self-check key at the back of this workbook.

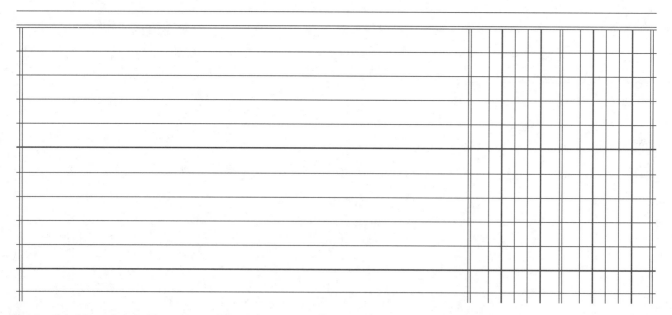

Project 1 (continued)

Name ______________________________

See the self-check key at the back of this workbook.

See the self-check key at the back of this workbook.

Extra Forms

Chapter 7

Name ______________________

Date ______________________

THE GENERAL JOURNAL

Exercise 7-1

Account Number	Account Name	Account Number	Account Name

Exercise 7-2

GENERAL JOURNAL PAGE ______

DATE		DESCRIPTION	POST. REF.	DEBIT	CREDIT

Exercise 7-3

GENERAL JOURNAL

PAGE ______

DATE		DESCRIPTION	POST. REF.	DEBIT	CREDIT

Problem 7-1

Name ____________________

GENERAL JOURNAL

PAGE ________

DATE		DESCRIPTION	POST. REF.	DEBIT	CREDIT

Note: Save the general journal for use in Problem 8-1.

Problem 7-1 (continued)

GENERAL JOURNAL PAGE ______

DATE		DESCRIPTION	POST. REF.	DEBIT	CREDIT

Note: Save the general journal for use in Problem 8-1.

Problem 7-1 (continued)

Name ______________________

GENERAL JOURNAL

PAGE ______

DATE		DESCRIPTION	POST. REF.	DEBIT	CREDIT

See the self-check key at the back of this workbook.

Note: Save the general journal for use in Problem 8-1.

Problem 7-2

GENERAL JOURNAL PAGE ________

DATE		DESCRIPTION	POST. REF.	DEBIT	CREDIT

Note: Save the general journal for use in Problem 8-2.

Problem 7-2 (continued)

Name ______________________________

GENERAL JOURNAL

PAGE ________

DATE	DESCRIPTION	POST. REF.	DEBIT	CREDIT

Note: Save the general journal for use in Problem 8-2.

Problem 7-2 (continued)

GENERAL JOURNAL

PAGE ______

DATE		DESCRIPTION	POST. REF.	DEBIT	CREDIT

See the self-check key at the back of this workbook.

Note: Save the general journal for use in Problem 8-2.

Case Study 7

Name ____________________

Extra Form

GENERAL JOURNAL

PAGE ______

DATE		DESCRIPTION	POST. REF.	DEBIT	CREDIT

Chapter 8

Name ______________________

Date ______________________

THE GENERAL LEDGER

Exercise 8-1

Cash — NO. 101

DATE		DESCRIPTION	POST REF.	DEBIT	CREDIT	BALANCE DEBIT	BALANCE CREDIT
20XX							
Jan	1	Balance	✓			16,000 00	
	5		J1		1,000 00		
	10		J1	2,000 00			
	15		J1		500 00		
	20		J1	1,500 00			
	30		J1		3,000 00		

Accounts Payable — NO. 201

DATE		DESCRIPTION	POST REF.	DEBIT	CREDIT	BALANCE DEBIT	BALANCE CREDIT
20XX							
Jan	3		J1		2,500 00		
	7		J1	500 00			
	14		J1	500 00			
	21		J1	500 00			
	28		J1		1,000 00		

Exercise 8-2

a. ______________________

b. ______________________

c. ______________________

d. ______________________

e. ______________________

Exercise 8-3

ACCT. NO.	ACCOUNT NAME	DEBIT	CREDIT

See the self-check key at the back of this workbook.

Note: Save the trial balance for use in Problem 9-1.

Problem 8-1

Name ______________________

______________________ NO. ______

DATE		DESCRIPTION	POST REF.	DEBIT	CREDIT	BALANCE	
						DEBIT	CREDIT

______________________ NO. ______

DATE		DESCRIPTION	POST REF.	DEBIT	CREDIT	BALANCE	
						DEBIT	CREDIT

Problem 8-1 (continued)

NO.

DATE		DESCRIPTION	POST REF.	DEBIT	CREDIT	BALANCE	
						DEBIT	CREDIT

NO.

DATE		DESCRIPTION	POST REF.	DEBIT	CREDIT	BALANCE	
						DEBIT	CREDIT

NO.

DATE		DESCRIPTION	POST REF.	DEBIT	CREDIT	BALANCE	
						DEBIT	CREDIT

NO.

DATE		DESCRIPTION	POST REF.	DEBIT	CREDIT	BALANCE	
						DEBIT	CREDIT

Problem 8-1 (continued)

Name ______________________

______________________ NO. ______

DATE		DESCRIPTION	POST REF.	DEBIT	CREDIT	BALANCE	
						DEBIT	CREDIT

______________________ NO. ______

DATE		DESCRIPTION	POST REF.	DEBIT	CREDIT	BALANCE	
						DEBIT	CREDIT

______________________ NO. ______

DATE		DESCRIPTION	POST REF.	DEBIT	CREDIT	BALANCE	
						DEBIT	CREDIT

______________________ NO. ______

DATE		DESCRIPTION	POST REF.	DEBIT	CREDIT	BALANCE	
						DEBIT	CREDIT

Problem 8-1 (continued)

NO.

DATE		DESCRIPTION	POST REF.	DEBIT	CREDIT	BALANCE	
						DEBIT	CREDIT

NO.

DATE		DESCRIPTION	POST REF.	DEBIT	CREDIT	BALANCE	
						DEBIT	CREDIT

NO.

DATE		DESCRIPTION	POST REF.	DEBIT	CREDIT	BALANCE	
						DEBIT	CREDIT

NO.

DATE		DESCRIPTION	POST REF.	DEBIT	CREDIT	BALANCE	
						DEBIT	CREDIT

Problem 8-1 (continued)

Name ______________________

ACCT. NO.	ACCOUNT NAME	DEBIT	CREDIT

See the self-check key at the back of this workbook.

Note: Save the trial balance for use in Problem 9-1.

Problem 8-2

NO. ______

DATE		DESCRIPTION	POST REF.	DEBIT	CREDIT	BALANCE DEBIT	BALANCE CREDIT

NO. ______

DATE		DESCRIPTION	POST REF.	DEBIT	CREDIT	BALANCE DEBIT	BALANCE CREDIT

Problem 8-2 (continued)

Name ______________________

______________________ NO. ______

DATE	DESCRIPTION	POST REF.	DEBIT	CREDIT	BALANCE	
					DEBIT	CREDIT

______________________ NO. ______

DATE	DESCRIPTION	POST REF.	DEBIT	CREDIT	BALANCE	
					DEBIT	CREDIT

______________________ NO. ______

DATE	DESCRIPTION	POST REF.	DEBIT	CREDIT	BALANCE	
					DEBIT	CREDIT

______________________ NO. ______

DATE	DESCRIPTION	POST REF.	DEBIT	CREDIT	BALANCE	
					DEBIT	CREDIT

NO. ______

DATE		DESCRIPTION	POST REF.	DEBIT	CREDIT	BALANCE	
						DEBIT	CREDIT

NO. ______

DATE		DESCRIPTION	POST REF.	DEBIT	CREDIT	BALANCE	
						DEBIT	CREDIT

NO. ______

DATE		DESCRIPTION	POST REF.	DEBIT	CREDIT	BALANCE	
						DEBIT	CREDIT

NO. ______

DATE		DESCRIPTION	POST REF.	DEBIT	CREDIT	BALANCE	
						DEBIT	CREDIT

Problem 8-2 (continued)

Name ______________________

______________________ NO. ________

DATE		DESCRIPTION	POST REF.	DEBIT	CREDIT	BALANCE	
						DEBIT	CREDIT

______________________ NO. ________

DATE		DESCRIPTION	POST REF.	DEBIT	CREDIT	BALANCE	
						DEBIT	CREDIT

______________________ NO. ________

DATE		DESCRIPTION	POST REF.	DEBIT	CREDIT	BALANCE	
						DEBIT	CREDIT

______________________ NO. ________

DATE		DESCRIPTION	POST REF.	DEBIT	CREDIT	BALANCE	
						DEBIT	CREDIT

Problem 8-2 (continued)

ACCT. NO.	ACCOUNT NAME	DEBIT	CREDIT

See the self-check key at the back of this workbook.

Note: Save the trial balance for use in Problem 9-2.

Case Study 8

Name ______________________________

Extra Form

NO.

DATE		DESCRIPTION	POST REF.	DEBIT	CREDIT	BALANCE	
						DEBIT	CREDIT

NO.

DATE		DESCRIPTION	POST REF.	DEBIT	CREDIT	BALANCE	
						DEBIT	CREDIT

NO.

DATE		DESCRIPTION	POST REF.	DEBIT	CREDIT	BALANCE	
						DEBIT	CREDIT

NO.

DATE		DESCRIPTION	POST REF.	DEBIT	CREDIT	BALANCE	
						DEBIT	CREDIT

Chapter 9

Name ______________________

Date ______________________

THE WORKSHEET AND THE FINANCIAL STATEMENTS

Exercise 9-1

ACCT. NO.	ACCOUNT NAME	TRIAL BALANCE		INCOME STATEMENT		BALANCE SHEET	
		DEBIT	CREDIT	DEBIT	CREDIT	DEBIT	CREDIT

Exercise 9-2

ACCT. NO.	ACCOUNT NAME	TRIAL BALANCE		INCOME STATEMENT		BALANCE SHEET	
		DEBIT	CREDIT	DEBIT	CREDIT	DEBIT	CREDIT

Exercise 9-3

Exercise 9-3 (continued)

Name ______________________

Exercise 9-4

Exercise 9-4 (continued)

Problem 9-1

Name ______________________

ACCT. NO.	ACCOUNT NAME	TRIAL BALANCE		INCOME STATEMENT		BALANCE SHEET	
		DEBIT	CREDIT	DEBIT	CREDIT	DEBIT	CREDIT

See the self-check key at the back of this workbook.
Note: Save the worksheet for use in Problem 10-1.

See the self-check key at the back of this workbook.

Problem 9-1 (continued)

See the self-check key at the back of this workbook.

See the self-check key at the back of this workbook.

Problem 9-2

Name ______________________

ACCT. NO.	ACCOUNT NAME	TRIAL BALANCE		INCOME STATEMENT		BALANCE SHEET	
		DEBIT	CREDIT	DEBIT	CREDIT	DEBIT	CREDIT

See the self-check key at the back of this workbook.

Note: Save the worksheet for use in Problem 10-2.

See the self-check key at the back of this workbook.

Problem 9-2 (continued)

See the self-check key at the back of this workbook.

See the self-check key at the back of this workbook.

Problem 9-3

Name ______________________________

ACCT. NO.	ACCOUNT NAME	TRIAL BALANCE		INCOME STATEMENT		BALANCE SHEET	
		DEBIT	CREDIT	DEBIT	CREDIT	DEBIT	CREDIT

See the self-check key at the back of this workbook.

See the self-check key at the back of this workbook.

Problem 9-3 (continued)

See the self-check key at the back of this workbook.

See the self-check key at the back of this workbook.

Case Study 9

Name

Extra Form

ACCT. NO.	ACCOUNT NAME	ADJUSTED TRIAL BALANCE		INCOME STATEMENT		BALANCE SHEET	
		DEBIT	CREDIT	DEBIT	CREDIT	DEBIT	CREDIT

Chapter 10

Name ______________________

Date ______________________

CLOSING THE LEDGER

Exercise 10-1

GENERAL JOURNAL

PAGE ______

DATE	DESCRIPTION	POST. REF.	DEBIT	CREDIT

Exercise 10-2

GENERAL JOURNAL PAGE ______

DATE		DESCRIPTION	POST. REF.	DEBIT	CREDIT

Name ______________________________

GENERAL JOURNAL

PAGE ________

DATE		DESCRIPTION	POST. REF.	DEBIT	CREDIT

Problem 10-1 (continued)

ACCT. NO.	ACCOUNT NAME	DEBIT	CREDIT

See the self-check key at the back of this workbook.

Problem 10-2

Name ______________________

GENERAL JOURNAL

PAGE ________

DATE		DESCRIPTION	POST. REF.	DEBIT	CREDIT

See the self-check key at the back of this workbook.

Problem 10-2 (continued)

ACCT. NO.	ACCOUNT NAME	DEBIT	CREDIT

See the self-check key at the back of this workbook.

Case Study 10

Name ______________________________

Extra Form

GENERAL JOURNAL

PAGE ______

DATE		DESCRIPTION	POST. REF.	DEBIT	CREDIT

PROJECT 2

Name ______________________

Date ______________________

GENERAL JOURNAL

PAGE ________

DATE		DESCRIPTION	POST. REF.	DEBIT	CREDIT

Project 2 (continued)

GENERAL JOURNAL PAGE ________

DATE		DESCRIPTION	POST. REF.	DEBIT	CREDIT

Project 2 (continued)

Name ______________________________

GENERAL JOURNAL

PAGE ________

DATE	DESCRIPTION	POST. REF.	DEBIT	CREDIT

GENERAL JOURNAL

PAGE ______

DATE		DESCRIPTION	POST. REF.	DEBIT	CREDIT

Name ______________________

NO. ______

DATE	DESCRIPTION	POST REF.	DEBIT	CREDIT	BALANCE	
					DEBIT	CREDIT

NO. ______

DATE	DESCRIPTION	POST REF.	DEBIT	CREDIT	BALANCE	
					DEBIT	CREDIT

Project 2 (continued)

NO. ______

DATE	DESCRIPTION	POST REF.	DEBIT	CREDIT	BALANCE	
					DEBIT	CREDIT

NO. ______

DATE	DESCRIPTION	POST REF.	DEBIT	CREDIT	BALANCE	
					DEBIT	CREDIT

NO. ______

DATE	DESCRIPTION	POST REF.	DEBIT	CREDIT	BALANCE	
					DEBIT	CREDIT

NO. ______

DATE	DESCRIPTION	POST REF.	DEBIT	CREDIT	BALANCE	
					DEBIT	CREDIT

Project 2 (continued)

Name ____________________

______________________________ NO. ______

DATE	DESCRIPTION	POST REF.	DEBIT	CREDIT	BALANCE	
					DEBIT	CREDIT

______________________________ NO. ______

DATE	DESCRIPTION	POST REF.	DEBIT	CREDIT	BALANCE	
					DEBIT	CREDIT

______________________________ NO. ______

DATE	DESCRIPTION	POST REF.	DEBIT	CREDIT	BALANCE	
					DEBIT	CREDIT

______________________________ NO. ______

DATE	DESCRIPTION	POST REF.	DEBIT	CREDIT	BALANCE	
					DEBIT	CREDIT

Project 2 (continued)

NO. ______

DATE	DESCRIPTION	POST REF.	DEBIT	CREDIT	BALANCE	
					DEBIT	CREDIT

NO. ______

DATE	DESCRIPTION	POST REF.	DEBIT	CREDIT	BALANCE	
					DEBIT	CREDIT

NO. ______

DATE	DESCRIPTION	POST REF.	DEBIT	CREDIT	BALANCE	
					DEBIT	CREDIT

NO. ______

DATE	DESCRIPTION	POST REF.	DEBIT	CREDIT	BALANCE	
					DEBIT	CREDIT

Project 2 (continued)

Name ______________________

______________________ NO. ______

DATE		DESCRIPTION	POST REF.	DEBIT	CREDIT	BALANCE	
						DEBIT	CREDIT

______________________ NO. ______

DATE		DESCRIPTION	POST REF.	DEBIT	CREDIT	BALANCE	
						DEBIT	CREDIT

______________________ NO. ______

DATE		DESCRIPTION	POST REF.	DEBIT	CREDIT	BALANCE	
						DEBIT	CREDIT

Project 2 (continued)

ACCT. NO.	ACCOUNT NAME	TRIAL BALANCE		INCOME STATEMENT		BALANCE SHEET	
		DEBIT	CREDIT	DEBIT	CREDIT	DEBIT	CREDIT

See the self-check key at the back of this workbook.

Project 2 (continued)

Name ______________________________

See the self-check key at the back of this workbook.

See the self-check key at the back of this workbook.

Project 2 (continued)

See the self-check key at the back of this workbook.

ACCT. NO.	ACCOUNT NAME	DEBIT	CREDIT

See the self-check key at the back of this workbook.

Chapter 11

Name ______________________

Date ______________________

INTRODUCTION TO MERCHANDISING BUSINESSES: SALES

Exercise 11-1

	Sale Amount	Sales Tax Percentage	Tax Amount	Total Sales Slip Amount
a.	$30.00	6%	______	______
b.	$60.00	8%	______	______
c.	$87.43	6%	______	______

Exercise 11-2

	Invoice Date	Terms	End of Discount Period
a.	May 10	2/10, n/30	______
b.	October 25	3/10, n/30	______
c.	June 30	3/10, n/30 EOM	______
d.	December 4	3/10, n/30 EOM	______

Problem 11-1

	Sales Slip Amount Excluding Sales Tax	6% Sales Tax	Total Sales Slip Amount
a.	$59.27	$	$
b.	34.26		
c.	87.98		
d.	2.59		

See the self-check key at the back of this workbook.

Problem 11-2

	Date of Invoice	Amount of Invoice	Last Day to Deduct Discount	Amount of Discount	Amount of Payment
a.	July 5	$197.46		$	$
b.	July 11	339.50			
c.	July 22	80.32			
d.	July 31	46.53			

See the self-check key at the back of this workbook.

Problem 11-3

1. ______________________________

2. ______________________________

3. ______________________________

4. ______________________________

5. ______________________________

See the self-check key at the back of this workbook.

Problem 11-4

Name ______________________

Instruction 1

	Date of Invoice	Amount of Invoice	Credit Terms	Last Day to Deduct Discount	Last Day for Payment
a.	Apr. 8	$ 650	n/30		
b.	June 14	1,800	2/10, n/30		
c.	Aug. 16	780	3/15, n/60		
d.	Sept 12	400	n/60		
e.	Oct. 16	980	2/10, n/30 EOM		
f.	Nov. 12	550	3/10, n/30 EOM		
g.	Jan. 22	670	1/10, n/30		

Instruction 2

	Date of Invoice	Amount of Invoice	Credit Terms	Date Paid	Amount of Discount	Amount of Payment	Check Here If Payment Was Late
a.	Apr. 8	$ 650	n/30	May 6	$	$	
b.	June 14	1,800	2/10, n/30	July 18			
c.	Aug. 16	780	3/15, n/60	Aug. 28			
d.	Sept 12	400	n/60	Oct. 31			
e.	Oct. 16	980	2/10, n/30 EOM	Nov. 7			
f.	Nov. 12	550	3/10, n/30 EOM	Dec. 8			
g.	Jan. 22	670	1/10, n/30	Jan. 30			

See the self-check key at the back of this workbook.

Case Study 11

Chapter 12

Name ______________________

Date ______________________

INTRODUCTION TO MERCHANDISING BUSINESSES: PURCHASES

Exercise 12-1

	Date of Invoice	Credit Terms	Last Date to Deduct Discount
a.	Jan. 6	n,30	________
b.	March 8	2/10, n/30	________
c.	July 17	2/15, n/60	________
d.	Aug. 7	3/10, n/30 EOM	________
e.	Aug. 20	2/10, n/30 EOM	________

Exercise 12-2

Invoice	Transportation	Who Pays
726	FOB Destination	________
409	FOB Shipping Point	________

Exercise 12-3

	Merchandise Purchases	Trans. Charges	Purchases Returns and Allowances	Terms	Amount of Discount	Amount of Payment
a.	$1,000	____	____	2/10, n/30	________	________
b.	1,000	$60	____	2/10, n/30	________	________
c.	1,000	____	$100	2/10, n/30	________	________
d.	1,000	60	100	2/10, n/30	________	________
e.	1,000	60	100	n/30	________	________

Problem 12-1

Laurel Distributors
1411 Madison Drive
Chicago, Illinois 60612

Sold to: Leonetti Furniture Store
Twining Bridge Road
Newton, PA 18940

DATE RECEIVED 6/4/X1
QUANTITIES/PRICES JGR
EXTENSIONS/TOTAL
APPROVED

Invoice No. 8386
Date: June 1, 20XX
Terms: 2/10, n/30
Order No. 518

QUANTITY	STOCK NO.	DESCRIPTION	UNIT PRICE	AMOUNT
3	1202L	Walnut coffee tables	$ 67.00	$201.00
1	1188G	Rosewood desk	110.00	110.00
4	1346L	Maple end tables	45.00	180.00
		TOTAL		$491.00

HOME FURNITURE CO.
125 Webster Road, Grand Rapids, Michigan 49503

DATE RECEIVED 6/5/X1
QUANTITIES/PRICES JGR
EXTENSIONS/TOTAL
APPROVED

INVOICE NO. 945

TO Leonetti Furniture Store
Twining Bridge Road
Newton, PA 18940

DATE 6/2/20XX
TERMS 1/10, n/30
PURCHASE ORDER NO. 522

QUANTITY	STOCK NO.	DESCRIPTION	UNIT PRICE	AMOUNT
2	069	Leather lounge chairs	$142.00	$284.00
4	082	Tweed club chairs	137.00	548.00
			TOTAL	$842.00

See the self-check key at the back of this workbook.

Problem 12-2

Name ______________________

Invoice No.	Date of Invoice	Amount of Invoice	Last Day to Deduct Discount	Amount of Discount	Amount of Payment
8386	June 1	$491.00	________	$________	$________
945	June 2	832.00	________	________	________

Case Study 12

Extra Form

GENERAL JOURNAL PAGE ________

DATE		DESCRIPTION	POST. REF.	DEBIT	CREDIT

Chapter 13

Name ____________________

Date ____________________

ACCOUNTING FOR PURCHASES

Exercise 13-1

	Accounts(s) Debited	Account(s) Credited
a.		
b.		
c.		
d.		
e.		
f.		
g.		
h.		

Exercise 13-2

Instructions 1-3

Exercise 13-2 (continued)

Instruction 4

ACCT. NO.	ACCOUNT NAME	DEBIT	CREDIT

Exercise 13-3

Instructions 1-3

Exercise 13-3 (continued)

Name ______________________

Instruction 4

ACCT. NO.	ACCOUNT NAME	DEBIT	CREDIT

Exercise 13-4

Instructions 1-3

Exercise 13-4 (continued)

Instruction 4

ACCT. NO.	ACCOUNT NAME	DEBIT	CREDIT

Problem 13-1

Name ______________________

______________________ NO. ______

DATE		DESCRIPTION	POST REF.	DEBIT	CREDIT	BALANCE	
						DEBIT	CREDIT

______________________ NO. ______

DATE		DESCRIPTION	POST REF.	DEBIT	CREDIT	BALANCE	
						DEBIT	CREDIT

______________________ NO. ______

DATE		DESCRIPTION	POST REF.	DEBIT	CREDIT	BALANCE	
						DEBIT	CREDIT

______________________ NO. ______

DATE		DESCRIPTION	POST REF.	DEBIT	CREDIT	BALANCE	
						DEBIT	CREDIT

Problem 13-1 (continued)

NO. ______

DATE		DESCRIPTION	POST REF.	DEBIT	CREDIT	BALANCE	
						DEBIT	CREDIT

NO. ______

DATE		DESCRIPTION	POST REF.	DEBIT	CREDIT	BALANCE	
						DEBIT	CREDIT

NO. ______

DATE		DESCRIPTION	POST REF.	DEBIT	CREDIT	BALANCE	
						DEBIT	CREDIT

Problem 13-1 (continued)

Name ______________________

GENERAL JOURNAL

PAGE ________

DATE		DESCRIPTION	POST. REF.	DEBIT	CREDIT

Problem 13-1 (continued)

GENERAL JOURNAL PAGE ________

DATE		DESCRIPTION	POST. REF.	DEBIT	CREDIT

ACCT. NO.	ACCOUNT NAME	DEBIT	CREDIT

See the self-check key at the back of this workbook.

Case Study 13

Name ______________________________

Extra Form

GENERAL JOURNAL PAGE ______

DATE		DESCRIPTION	POST. REF.	DEBIT	CREDIT

ACCT. NO.	ACCOUNT NAME	DEBIT	CREDIT

Chapter 14

ACCOUNTING FOR SALES

Name ______________________

Date ______________________

Exercise 14-1

	Account(s) Debited	Account(s) Credited
a.		
b.		
c.		
d.		
e.		
f.		

Exercise 14-2

	Account(s) Debited	Account(s) Credited
a.		
b.		
c.		
d.		
e.		

Exercise 14-3

Instructions 1-3

Exercise 14-3 (continued)

Instruction 4

ACCT. NO.	ACCOUNT NAME	DEBIT	CREDIT

Exercise 14-4

Instructions 1-3

Instruction 4

Proof

ACCOUNT NAME	DEBIT	CREDIT

Problem 14-1

Name ______________________________

______________________________ NO. ________

DATE	DESCRIPTION	POST REF.	DEBIT	CREDIT	BALANCE	
					DEBIT	CREDIT

______________________________ NO. ________

DATE	DESCRIPTION	POST REF.	DEBIT	CREDIT	BALANCE	
					DEBIT	CREDIT

______________________________ NO. ________

DATE	DESCRIPTION	POST REF.	DEBIT	CREDIT	BALANCE	
					DEBIT	CREDIT

Problem 14-1 (continued)

NO. __________

DATE		DESCRIPTION	POST REF.	DEBIT	CREDIT	BALANCE	
						DEBIT	CREDIT

NO. __________

DATE		DESCRIPTION	POST REF.	DEBIT	CREDIT	BALANCE	
						DEBIT	CREDIT

NO. __________

DATE		DESCRIPTION	POST REF.	DEBIT	CREDIT	BALANCE	
						DEBIT	CREDIT

Name ______________________

GENERAL JOURNAL

PAGE ______

DATE		DESCRIPTION	POST. REF.	DEBIT	CREDIT

Problem 14-1 (continued)

GENERAL JOURNAL

PAGE ______

DATE		DESCRIPTION	POST. REF.	DEBIT	CREDIT

ACCT. NO.	ACCOUNT NAME	DEBIT	CREDIT

See the self-check key at the back of this workbook.

Case Study 14

Name ____________________

Extra Form

GENERAL JOURNAL

PAGE ________

DATE		DESCRIPTION	POST. REF.	DEBIT	CREDIT

ACCT. NO.	ACCOUNT NAME	DEBIT	CREDIT

Chapter 15

THE SALES JOURNAL

Name ______________________

Date ______________________

Exercise 15-1

Exercise 15-2

Exercise 15-3

Exercise 15-4

a.

b.

c.

Problem 15-1

SALES JOURNAL for Month of ____________ 20 ____ PAGE ____

DATE		INV. NO.	CUSTOMER'S ACCOUNT	ACCOUNTS RECEIVABLE ✓	ACCOUNTS RECEIVABLE DEBIT	SALES TAX PAYABLE CREDIT	SALES CREDIT

See the self-check key at the back of this workbook.
Note: Save this journal for use in Problem 15-2.

GENERAL JOURNAL PAGE ____

DATE		DESCRIPTION	POST. REF.	DEBIT	CREDIT

See the self-check key at the back of this workbook.
Note: Save this journal for use in Problem 15-2.

Problem 15-2

Name ____________________

____________________ NO. ______

DATE		DESCRIPTION	POST REF.	DEBIT	CREDIT	BALANCE	
						DEBIT	CREDIT

____________________ NO. ______

DATE		DESCRIPTION	POST REF.	DEBIT	CREDIT	BALANCE	
						DEBIT	CREDIT

____________________ NO. ______

DATE		DESCRIPTION	POST REF.	DEBIT	CREDIT	BALANCE	
						DEBIT	CREDIT

____________________ NO. ______

DATE		DESCRIPTION	POST REF.	DEBIT	CREDIT	BALANCE	
						DEBIT	CREDIT

Problem 15-2 (continued)

NO. ______

DATE		DESCRIPTION	POST REF.	DEBIT	CREDIT	BALANCE	
						DEBIT	CREDIT

NO. ______

DATE		DESCRIPTION	POST REF.	DEBIT	CREDIT	BALANCE	
						DEBIT	CREDIT

ACCT. NO.	ACCOUNT NAME	DEBIT	CREDIT

See the self-check key at the back of this workbook.

Case Study 15

Name ______________________________

Extra Forms

NO.

DATE	DESCRIPTION	POST REF.	DEBIT	CREDIT	BALANCE	
					DEBIT	CREDIT

NO.

DATE	DESCRIPTION	POST REF.	DEBIT	CREDIT	BALANCE	
					DEBIT	CREDIT

NO.

DATE	DESCRIPTION	POST REF.	DEBIT	CREDIT	BALANCE	
					DEBIT	CREDIT

NO.

DATE	DESCRIPTION	POST REF.	DEBIT	CREDIT	BALANCE	
					DEBIT	CREDIT

Chapter 16

Name ______________________________

Date______________________________

THE PURCHASES JOURNAL

Exercise 16-1

____

____

Exercise 16-2

____

____

____

____

Exercise 16-3

____

____

Exercise 16-4

a. ____

____

b. ____

____

c. ____

____

Problem 16-1

GENERAL JOURNAL PAGE ______

DATE		DESCRIPTION	POST. REF.	DEBIT	CREDIT

Note: Save this journal for use in Problem 16-2.

Problem 16-1 (continued)

Name ______________________

PURCHASES JOURNAL for Month of ______________________ 20 ____ PAGE ____

DATE		CREDITOR'S ACCOUNT CREDITED	POST REF.	INVOICE NUMBER	INV. DATE	TERMS	ACCOUNTS PAYABLE CREDIT	MERCH. PURCHASES DEBIT	FREIGHT IN DEBIT

See the self-check key at the back of this workbook.
Note: Save this journal for use in Problem 16-2.

Problem 16-2

______________________ NO. ____

DATE		DESCRIPTION	POST REF.	DEBIT	CREDIT	BALANCE	
						DEBIT	CREDIT

______________________ NO. ____

DATE		DESCRIPTION	POST REF.	DEBIT	CREDIT	BALANCE	
						DEBIT	CREDIT

Problem 16-2 (continued)

NO. ______

DATE		DESCRIPTION	POST REF.	DEBIT	CREDIT	BALANCE	
						DEBIT	CREDIT

NO. ______

DATE		DESCRIPTION	POST REF.	DEBIT	CREDIT	BALANCE	
						DEBIT	CREDIT

NO. ______

DATE		DESCRIPTION	POST REF.	DEBIT	CREDIT	BALANCE	
						DEBIT	CREDIT

NO. ______

DATE		DESCRIPTION	POST REF.	DEBIT	CREDIT	BALANCE	
						DEBIT	CREDIT

Problem 16-2 (continued)

Name ____________________

______________________________ NO. ______

DATE		DESCRIPTION	POST REF.	DEBIT	CREDIT	BALANCE	
						DEBIT	CREDIT

______________________________ NO. ______

DATE		DESCRIPTION	POST REF.	DEBIT	CREDIT	BALANCE	
						DEBIT	CREDIT

ACCT. NO.	ACCOUNT NAME	DEBIT	CREDIT

Case Study 16

Chapter 17

Name ____________________

Date ____________________

THE CASH RECEIPTS JOURNAL

Exercise 17-1

a. ____________________

b. ____________________

c. ____________________

d. ____________________

e. ____________________

Exercise 17-2

	Journal	Account(s) Debited	Account(s) Credited
1.			
2.			
3.			
4.			
5.			
6.			
7.			
8.			
9.			
10.			

Exercise 17-3

Exercise 17-3 (continued)

Name ______________________________

ACCT. NO.	ACCOUNT NAME	DEBIT	CREDIT

Problem 17-1

NO.

DATE		DESCRIPTION	POST REF.	DEBIT	CREDIT	BALANCE	
						DEBIT	CREDIT

NO.

DATE		DESCRIPTION	POST REF.	DEBIT	CREDIT	BALANCE	
						DEBIT	CREDIT

NO.

DATE		DESCRIPTION	POST REF.	DEBIT	CREDIT	BALANCE	
						DEBIT	CREDIT

NO.

DATE		DESCRIPTION	POST REF.	DEBIT	CREDIT	BALANCE	
						DEBIT	CREDIT

NO.

DATE		DESCRIPTION	POST REF.	DEBIT	CREDIT	BALANCE	
						DEBIT	CREDIT

NO.

DATE		DESCRIPTION	POST REF.	DEBIT	CREDIT	BALANCE	
						DEBIT	CREDIT

Problem 17-1 (continued)

Name ______________________

CASH RECEIPTS JOURNAL for Month of ______________ 20 ___ PAGE ___

DATE	EXPLANATION	ACCOUNTS RECEIVABLE ✓	ACCOUNTS RECEIVABLE CREDIT	SALES TAX PAYABLE CREDIT	SALES CREDIT	OTHER ACCOUNTS CREDIT ACCOUNT NAME	OTHER ACCOUNTS CREDIT POST REF.	OTHER ACCOUNTS CREDIT AMOUNT	SALES DISCOUNT DEBIT	CASH DEBIT

See the self-check key at the back of this workbook.

Problem 17-1 (continued)

ACCT. NO.	ACCOUNT NAME	DEBIT	CREDIT

See the self-check key at the back of this workbook.

Problem 17-2

GENERAL JOURNAL PAGE ______

DATE		DESCRIPTION	POST. REF.	DEBIT	CREDIT

Problem 17-2 (continued)

Name ______________________

CASH RECEIPTS JOURNAL for Month of ______________ 20 ___ PAGE ___

DATE	EXPLANATION	ACCOUNTS RECEIVABLE		SALES TAX PAYABLE CREDIT	SALES CREDIT	OTHER ACCOUNTS CREDIT			SALES DISCOUNT DEBIT	CASH DEBIT
		✓	CREDIT			ACCOUNT NAME	POST REF.	AMOUNT		

See the self-check key at the back of this workbook.

Problem 17-2 (continued)

SALES JOURNAL for Month of ____________ 20 ____ PAGE ____

DATE		INV. NO.	CUSTOMER'S ACCOUNT	ACCOUNTS RECEIVABLE ✓	ACCOUNTS RECEIVABLE DEBIT	SALES TAX PAYABLE CREDIT	SALES CREDIT

See the self-check key at the back of this workbook.

____________ NO. ____

DATE		DESCRIPTION	POST REF.	DEBIT	CREDIT	BALANCE DEBIT	BALANCE CREDIT

____________ NO. ____

DATE		DESCRIPTION	POST REF.	DEBIT	CREDIT	BALANCE DEBIT	BALANCE CREDIT

____________ NO. ____

DATE		DESCRIPTION	POST REF.	DEBIT	CREDIT	BALANCE DEBIT	BALANCE CREDIT

Problem 17-2 (continued)

Name ____________________

______________________________ NO. ______

DATE		DESCRIPTION	POST REF.	DEBIT	CREDIT	BALANCE	
						DEBIT	CREDIT

______________________________ NO. ______

DATE		DESCRIPTION	POST REF.	DEBIT	CREDIT	BALANCE	
						DEBIT	CREDIT

______________________________ NO. ______

DATE		DESCRIPTION	POST REF.	DEBIT	CREDIT	BALANCE	
						DEBIT	CREDIT

____

____

____

ACCT. NO.	ACCOUNT NAME	DEBIT	CREDIT

See the self-check key at the back of this workbook.

Case Study 17

Chapter 18

Name ____________________

Date ____________________

THE CASH PAYMENTS JOURNAL

Exercise 18-1

a. ____________________

b. ____________________

c. ____________________

d. ____________________

e. ____________________

Exercise 18-2

	Debits	Credits
1.		
2.		
3.		
4.		
5.		

Exercise 18-3

	Journal	Account(s) Debited	Account(s) Credited
1.			
2.			
3.			
4.			
5.			
6.			
7.			
8.			
9.			
10.			
11.			
12.			
13.			
14.			

Problem 18-1

CASH PAYMENTS JOURNAL for Month of ____________ 20 ____ PAGE ____

DATE	CHECK NO.	EXPLANATION	ACCOUNTS PAYABLE		MERCHANDISE PURCHASES DEBIT	OTHER ACCOUNTS DEBIT			PUCHASES DISCOUNT CREDIT	CASH CREDIT
			✓	DEBIT		ACCOUNT NAME	POST REF.	AMOUNT		

See the self-check key at the back of this workbook.

Problem 18-2

Name ______________________

CASH PAYMENTS JOURNAL for Month of ______________ 20 ____ PAGE ____

DATE	CHECK NO.	EXPLANATION	ACCOUNTS PAYABLE ✓	ACCOUNTS PAYABLE DEBIT	MERCHANDISE PURCHASES DEBIT	OTHER ACCOUNTS DEBIT: ACCOUNT NAME	OTHER ACCOUNTS DEBIT: POST REF.	OTHER ACCOUNTS DEBIT: AMOUNT	PUCHASES DISCOUNT CREDIT	CASH CREDIT

See the self-check key at the back of this workbook.

Problem 18-2 (continued)

NO. ______

DATE		DESCRIPTION	POST REF.	DEBIT	CREDIT	BALANCE	
						DEBIT	CREDIT

NO. ______

DATE		DESCRIPTION	POST REF.	DEBIT	CREDIT	BALANCE	
						DEBIT	CREDIT

NO. ______

DATE		DESCRIPTION	POST REF.	DEBIT	CREDIT	BALANCE	
						DEBIT	CREDIT

Name ______________________

______________________ NO. ______

DATE		DESCRIPTION	POST REF.	DEBIT	CREDIT	BALANCE	
						DEBIT	CREDIT

______________________ NO. ______

DATE		DESCRIPTION	POST REF.	DEBIT	CREDIT	BALANCE	
						DEBIT	CREDIT

______________________ NO. ______

DATE		DESCRIPTION	POST REF.	DEBIT	CREDIT	BALANCE	
						DEBIT	CREDIT

______________________ NO. ______

DATE		DESCRIPTION	POST REF.	DEBIT	CREDIT	BALANCE	
						DEBIT	CREDIT

Problem 18-2 (continued)

NO. ______

DATE		DESCRIPTION	POST REF.	DEBIT	CREDIT	BALANCE	
						DEBIT	CREDIT

NO. ______

DATE		DESCRIPTION	POST REF.	DEBIT	CREDIT	BALANCE	
						DEBIT	CREDIT

NO. ______

DATE		DESCRIPTION	POST REF.	DEBIT	CREDIT	BALANCE	
						DEBIT	CREDIT

NO. ______

DATE		DESCRIPTION	POST REF.	DEBIT	CREDIT	BALANCE	
						DEBIT	CREDIT

NO. ______

DATE		DESCRIPTION	POST REF.	DEBIT	CREDIT	BALANCE	
						DEBIT	CREDIT

Name ______________________

______________________ NO. ________

DATE		DESCRIPTION	POST REF.	DEBIT	CREDIT	BALANCE DEBIT	BALANCE CREDIT

ACCT. NO.	ACCOUNT NAME	DEBIT	CREDIT

See the self-check key at the back of this workbook.

Case Study 18

Chapter 19

Name ______________________

Date ______________________

THE ACCOUNTS RECEIVABLE LEDGER

Exercise 19-1

General Ledger

Accounts Receivable Ledger

CUSTOMER	BALANCE

Exercise 19-2

NAME ______________________

ADDRESS ______________________

______________________ TERMS: ________

DATE		DESCRIPTION	POST. REF.	DEBIT	CREDIT	BALANCE

Exercise 19-3

Forest Grove Distributing					
Schedule of Accounts Receivable by Age					
April 30, 20XX					
Customer	Balance	Current	Past Due		
			1–30 Days	31–60 Days	Over 60 Days

Exercise 19-4

Instruction 1

Instruction 3

Proof

	Debit	Credit

Problem 19-1

Name ____________________

NAME ____________________

ADDRESS ____________________

____________________ TERMS: __________

DATE		DESCRIPTION	POST. REF.	DEBIT	CREDIT	BALANCE

Problem 19-2

GENERAL JOURNAL PAGE ______

DATE		DESCRIPTION	POST. REF.	DEBIT	CREDIT

Problem 19-2 (continued)

CASH RECEIPTS JOURNAL for Month of ______________________ 20 ______ PAGE ______

DATE	EXPLANATION	ACCOUNTS RECEIVABLE		SALES TAX PAYABLE CREDIT	SALES CREDIT	OTHER ACCOUNTS CREDIT			SALES DISCOUNT DEBIT	CASH DEBIT
		✓	CREDIT			ACCOUNT NAME	POST REF.	AMOUNT		

See the self-check key at the back of this workbook.

Problem 19-2 (continued)

Name ______________________

SALES JOURNAL for Month of ______________________ 20 ____ PAGE ____

DATE		INV. NO.	CUSTOMER'S ACCOUNT	ACCOUNTS RECEIVABLE		SALES TAX PAYABLE CREDIT	SALES CREDIT
				✓	DEBIT		

See the self-check key at the back of this workbook.

______________________ NO. ____

DATE		DESCRIPTION	POST REF.	DEBIT	CREDIT	BALANCE	
						DEBIT	CREDIT

______________________ NO. ____

DATE		DESCRIPTION	POST REF.	DEBIT	CREDIT	BALANCE	
						DEBIT	CREDIT

______________________ NO. ____

DATE		DESCRIPTION	POST REF.	DEBIT	CREDIT	BALANCE	
						DEBIT	CREDIT

Problem 19-2 (continued)

NO. ______

DATE		DESCRIPTION	POST REF.	DEBIT	CREDIT	BALANCE	
						DEBIT	CREDIT

NO. ______

DATE		DESCRIPTION	POST REF.	DEBIT	CREDIT	BALANCE	
						DEBIT	CREDIT

NO. ______

DATE		DESCRIPTION	POST REF.	DEBIT	CREDIT	BALANCE	
						DEBIT	CREDIT

NO. ______

DATE		DESCRIPTION	POST REF.	DEBIT	CREDIT	BALANCE	
						DEBIT	CREDIT

ACCOUNTS RECEIVABLE LEDGER

NAME ______

ADDRESS ______

______ TERMS: ______

DATE		DESCRIPTION	POST. REF.	DEBIT	CREDIT	BALANCE

 Name ______________________

NAME ______________________

ADDRESS ______________________

______________________ TERMS: __________

DATE		DESCRIPTION	POST. REF.	DEBIT	CREDIT	BALANCE

NAME ______________________

ADDRESS ______________________

______________________ TERMS: __________

DATE		DESCRIPTION	POST. REF.	DEBIT	CREDIT	BALANCE

NAME ______________________

ADDRESS ______________________

______________________ TERMS: __________

DATE		DESCRIPTION	POST. REF.	DEBIT	CREDIT	BALANCE

Problem 19-2 (continued)

CUSTOMER	BALANCE

STATEMENT OF ACCOUNT

Wing Lu Packaging
675 Main Avenue
Greenville, Pennsylvania 16125

DATE

DATE	DESCRIPTION	CHARGES	CREDITS	BALANCE

See the self-check key at the back of this workbook.

Case Study 19

Name ______________________

CASH RECEIPTS JOURNAL for Month of ______________ 20 ____ PAGE ____

DATE	EXPLANATION	ACCOUNTS RECEIVABLE		SALES TAX PAYABLE CREDIT	SALES CREDIT	OTHER ACCOUNTS CREDIT			SALES DISCOUNT DEBIT	CASH DEBIT
		✓	CREDIT			ACCOUNT NAME	POST REF.	AMOUNT		

Name ______________________________

Date ______________________________

Chapter 20

THE ACCOUNTS PAYABLE LEDGER

Exercise 20-1

General Ledger

Accounts Payable Ledger

CREDITOR	BALANCE

Exercise 20-2

NAME ______________________________

ADDRESS ______________________________

______________________________ TERMS: __________

DATE	DESCRIPTION	POST. REF.	DEBIT	CREDIT	BALANCE

Exercise 20-3

	Journal	Accounts Receivable	Accounts Payable
1.			
2.			
3.			
4.			
5.			
6.			
7.			
8.			
9.			
10.			

Exercise 20-4

Name ______________________________

ACCT. NO.	ACCOUNT NAME	DEBIT	CREDIT

Problem 20-1

NAME ______________________________

ADDRESS ______________________________

______________________________ TERMS: __________

DATE		DESCRIPTION	POST. REF.	DEBIT	CREDIT	BALANCE

See the self-check key at the back of this workbook.

Problem 20-2

GENERAL JOURNAL PAGE __________

DATE		DESCRIPTION	POST. REF.	DEBIT	CREDIT

 Name ______________________

CASH PAYMENTS JOURNAL for Month of ______________ 20 ___ PAGE ___

DATE	CHECK NO.	EXPLANATION	ACCOUNTS PAYABLE ✓	ACCOUNTS PAYABLE DEBIT	MERCHANDISE PURCHASES DEBIT	OTHER ACCOUNTS DEBIT ACCOUNT NAME	OTHER ACCOUNTS DEBIT POST REF.	OTHER ACCOUNTS DEBIT AMOUNT	PURCHASES DISCOUNT CREDIT	CASH CREDIT

See the self-check key at the back of this workbook.

Problem 20-2 (continued)

PURCHASES JOURNAL for Month of ______________ 20 ____ PAGE ____

DATE		CREDITOR'S ACCOUNT CREDITED	POST REF.	INVOICE NUMBER	INV. DATE	TERMS	ACCOUNTS PAYABLE CREDIT	MERCH. PURCHASES DEBIT	FREIGHT IN DEBIT

See the self-check key at the back of this workbook.

______________________________ NO. ______

DATE		DESCRIPTION	POST REF.	DEBIT	CREDIT	BALANCE	
						DEBIT	CREDIT

______________________________ NO. ______

DATE		DESCRIPTION	POST REF.	DEBIT	CREDIT	BALANCE	
						DEBIT	CREDIT

______________________________ NO. ______

DATE		DESCRIPTION	POST REF.	DEBIT	CREDIT	BALANCE	
						DEBIT	CREDIT

 Name ______

______ NO. ____

DATE		DESCRIPTION	POST REF.	DEBIT	CREDIT	BALANCE	
						DEBIT	CREDIT

______ NO. ____

DATE		DESCRIPTION	POST REF.	DEBIT	CREDIT	BALANCE	
						DEBIT	CREDIT

______ NO. ____

DATE		DESCRIPTION	POST REF.	DEBIT	CREDIT	BALANCE	
						DEBIT	CREDIT

______ NO. ____

DATE		DESCRIPTION	POST REF.	DEBIT	CREDIT	BALANCE	
						DEBIT	CREDIT

______ NO. ____

DATE		DESCRIPTION	POST REF.	DEBIT	CREDIT	BALANCE	
						DEBIT	CREDIT

Problem 20-2 (continued)

ACCOUNTS PAYABLE LEDGER

NAME ______________________

ADDRESS ______________________

______________________ TERMS: ________

DATE		DESCRIPTION	POST. REF.	DEBIT	CREDIT	BALANCE

NAME ______________________

ADDRESS ______________________

______________________ TERMS: ________

DATE		DESCRIPTION	POST. REF.	DEBIT	CREDIT	BALANCE

NAME ______________________

ADDRESS ______________________

______________________ TERMS: ________

DATE		DESCRIPTION	POST. REF.	DEBIT	CREDIT	BALANCE

Problem 20-2 (continued)

Name ______________________

NAME ______________________

ADDRESS ______________________

______________________ TERMS: __________

DATE		DESCRIPTION	POST. REF.	DEBIT	CREDIT	BALANCE

CREDITOR	BALANCE

See the self-check key at the back of this workbook.

Case Study 20

PROJECT 3

Name ______________________

Date ______________________

GENERAL JOURNAL

PAGE ______

DATE		DESCRIPTION	POST. REF.	DEBIT	CREDIT

CASH RECEIPTS JOURNAL for Month of ______________ 20 ____ PAGE ____

DATE	EXPLANATION	ACCOUNTS RECEIVABLE		SALES TAX PAYABLE CREDIT	SALES CREDIT	OTHER ACCOUNTS CREDIT			SALES DISCOUNT DEBIT	CASH DEBIT
		✓	CREDIT			ACCOUNT NAME	POST REF.	AMOUNT		

See the self-check key at the back of this workbook.

Project 3 (continued)

Name ______________________________

CASH PAYMENTS JOURNAL for Month of ______________ 20____ PAGE ____

DATE	CHECK NO.	EXPLANATION	ACCOUNTS PAYABLE ✓	ACCOUNTS PAYABLE DEBIT	MERCHANDISE PURCHASES DEBIT	OTHER ACCOUNTS DEBIT ACCOUNT NAME	OTHER ACCOUNTS DEBIT POST REF.	OTHER ACCOUNTS DEBIT AMOUNT	PURCHASES DISCOUNT CREDIT	CASH CREDIT

See the self-check key at the back of this workbook.

Project 3 (continued)

SALES JOURNAL for Month of ______________ 20 ____ PAGE ____

DATE		INV. NO.	CUSTOMER'S ACCOUNT	ACCOUNTS RECEIVABLE		SALES TAX PAYABLE CREDIT	SALES CREDIT
				✓	DEBIT		

See the self-check key at the back of this workbook.

PURCHASES JOURNAL for Month of ______________ 20 ____ PAGE ____

DATE		CREDITOR'S ACCOUNT CREDITED	POST REF.	INVOICE NUMBER	INV. DATE	TERMS	ACCOUNTS PAYABLE CREDIT	MERCH. PURCHASES DEBIT	FREIGHT IN DEBIT

See the self-check key at the back of this workbook.

Project 3 (continued)

Name ______________________

Cash NO. 101

DATE	DESCRIPTION	POST REF.	DEBIT	CREDIT	BALANCE	
					DEBIT	CREDIT

Accounts Receivable NO. 112

DATE	DESCRIPTION	POST REF.	DEBIT	CREDIT	BALANCE	
					DEBIT	CREDIT

Allowance for Uncollectible Accounts NO. 113

DATE	DESCRIPTION	POST REF.	DEBIT	CREDIT	BALANCE	
					DEBIT	CREDIT

Merchandise Inventory NO. 114

DATE	DESCRIPTION	POST REF.	DEBIT	CREDIT	BALANCE	
					DEBIT	CREDIT

Supplies NO. 115

DATE	DESCRIPTION	POST REF.	DEBIT	CREDIT	BALANCE	
					DEBIT	CREDIT

Project 3 (continued)

Prepaid Insurance NO. 116

DATE	DESCRIPTION	POST REF.	DEBIT	CREDIT	BALANCE	
					DEBIT	CREDIT

Office Equipment NO. 126

DATE	DESCRIPTION	POST REF.	DEBIT	CREDIT	BALANCE	
					DEBIT	CREDIT

Accumulated Depreciation — Office Equipment NO. 127

DATE	DESCRIPTION	POST REF.	DEBIT	CREDIT	BALANCE	
					DEBIT	CREDIT

Warehouse Equipment NO. 128

DATE	DESCRIPTION	POST REF.	DEBIT	CREDIT	BALANCE	
					DEBIT	CREDIT

Accumulated Depreciation — Warehouse Equipment NO. 129

DATE	DESCRIPTION	POST REF.	DEBIT	CREDIT	BALANCE	
					DEBIT	CREDIT

Project 3 (continued)

Name ____________________

Accounts Payable — NO. 202

DATE	DESCRIPTION	POST REF.	DEBIT	CREDIT	BALANCE	
					DEBIT	CREDIT

Sales Tax Payable — NO. 231

DATE	DESCRIPTION	POST REF.	DEBIT	CREDIT	BALANCE	
					DEBIT	CREDIT

Anthony Leeser, Capital — NO. 301

DATE	DESCRIPTION	POST REF.	DEBIT	CREDIT	BALANCE	
					DEBIT	CREDIT

Anthony Leeser, Withdrawals — NO. 302

DATE	DESCRIPTION	POST REF.	DEBIT	CREDIT	BALANCE	
					DEBIT	CREDIT

Project 3 (continued)

Income Summary NO. 399

DATE		DESCRIPTION	POST REF.	DEBIT	CREDIT	BALANCE	
						DEBIT	CREDIT

Sales NO. 401

DATE		DESCRIPTION	POST REF.	DEBIT	CREDIT	BALANCE	
						DEBIT	CREDIT

Sales Returns and Allowances NO. 402

DATE		DESCRIPTION	POST REF.	DEBIT	CREDIT	BALANCE	
						DEBIT	CREDIT

Sales Discount NO. 403

DATE		DESCRIPTION	POST REF.	DEBIT	CREDIT	BALANCE	
						DEBIT	CREDIT

Name ____________________

Merchandise Purchases NO. 501

DATE		DESCRIPTION	POST REF.	DEBIT	CREDIT	BALANCE	
						DEBIT	CREDIT

Freight In NO. 502

DATE		DESCRIPTION	POST REF.	DEBIT	CREDIT	BALANCE	
						DEBIT	CREDIT

Purchases Returns and Allowances NO. 503

DATE		DESCRIPTION	POST REF.	DEBIT	CREDIT	BALANCE	
						DEBIT	CREDIT

Purchases Discount NO. 504

DATE		DESCRIPTION	POST REF.	DEBIT	CREDIT	BALANCE	
						DEBIT	CREDIT

Advertising Expense NO. 511

DATE		DESCRIPTION	POST REF.	DEBIT	CREDIT	BALANCE	
						DEBIT	CREDIT

Project 3 (continued)

Telephone Expense NO. 512

DATE		DESCRIPTION	POST REF.	DEBIT	CREDIT	BALANCE	
						DEBIT	CREDIT

Depreciation Expense — Office Equipment NO. 513

DATE		DESCRIPTION	POST REF.	DEBIT	CREDIT	BALANCE	
						DEBIT	CREDIT

Depreciation Expense — Warehouse Equipment NO. 514

DATE		DESCRIPTION	POST REF.	DEBIT	CREDIT	BALANCE	
						DEBIT	CREDIT

Rent Expense NO. 516

DATE		DESCRIPTION	POST REF.	DEBIT	CREDIT	BALANCE	
						DEBIT	CREDIT

Supplies Expense NO. 517

DATE		DESCRIPTION	POST REF.	DEBIT	CREDIT	BALANCE	
						DEBIT	CREDIT

Project 3 (continued)

Name ______________________

Utilities Expense NO. 518

DATE		DESCRIPTION	POST REF.	DEBIT	CREDIT	BALANCE DEBIT	BALANCE CREDIT

Wages Expense NO. 519

DATE		DESCRIPTION	POST REF.	DEBIT	CREDIT	BALANCE DEBIT	BALANCE CREDIT

Uncollectible Accounts Expense NO. 521

DATE		DESCRIPTION	POST REF.	DEBIT	CREDIT	BALANCE DEBIT	BALANCE CREDIT

Insurance Expense NO. 522

DATE		DESCRIPTION	POST REF.	DEBIT	CREDIT	BALANCE DEBIT	BALANCE CREDIT

Note: Save your general ledger for Project 4.

Project 3 (continued)

ACCOUNTS RECEIVABLE LEDGER

NAME Betterbuilt Homes
ADDRESS 2418 West Avenue
Ocean City, NJ 08226
TERMS: 2/10, n/30

DATE		DESCRIPTION	POST. REF.	DEBIT	CREDIT	BALANCE

NAME Cross Country Construction
ADDRESS 216 Northern Expressway
San Diego, CA 92112
TERMS: 2/10, n/30

DATE		DESCRIPTION	POST. REF.	DEBIT	CREDIT	BALANCE

NAME Archibald Builders
ADDRESS Greentree Road
Harrisburg, PA 17112
TERMS: 2/10, n/30

DATE		DESCRIPTION	POST. REF.	DEBIT	CREDIT	BALANCE

 Name ____________

NAME McKnight Developers
ADDRESS 5001 Marshall Street
San Diego, CA 92105
TERMS: 1/10, n/60

DATE		DESCRIPTION	POST. REF.	DEBIT	CREDIT	BALANCE

NAME Jorga Construction Company
ADDRESS 49 Thornridge Drive
Levittown, PA 19054
TERMS: 1/10, n/60

DATE		DESCRIPTION	POST. REF.	DEBIT	CREDIT	BALANCE

ACCOUNTS PAYABLE LEDGER

NAME Pine Forest Products
ADDRESS 9432 Taylor Road
Anchorage, AK 99516
TERMS: 2/10, n/30

DATE		DESCRIPTION	POST. REF.	DEBIT	CREDIT	BALANCE

Project 3 (continued)

NAME Bay Building Materials
ADDRESS 517 Highland Drive
Portland, OR 97211
TERMS: n/30

DATE		DESCRIPTION	POST. REF.	DEBIT	CREDIT	BALANCE

NAME Mountain Lumber Company
ADDRESS 46 Fairfax Avenue
Denver, CO 80239
TERMS: 1/30, n/60

DATE		DESCRIPTION	POST. REF.	DEBIT	CREDIT	BALANCE

NAME Sierra Wood Products
ADDRESS Plaza Center — Building 2A
San Francisco, CA 94124
TERMS: 2/10, n/30

DATE		DESCRIPTION	POST. REF.	DEBIT	CREDIT	BALANCE

Project 3 (continued)

Name ______________________________

CUSTOMER	BALANCE

See the self-check key at the back of this workbook.

CREDITOR	BALANCE

See the self-check key at the back of this workbook.

Project 3 (continued)

ACCT. NO.	ACCOUNT NAME	DEBIT	CREDIT

See the self-check key at the back of this workbook.
Note: Save your trial balance for use in Project 4.

Chapter 21

Name ______________________

Date ______________________

WORKSHEET ADJUSTMENTS

Exercise 21-1

GENERAL JOURNAL PAGE ______

DATE		DESCRIPTION	POST. REF.	DEBIT	CREDIT

Exercise 21-2

a. ______________________

____

b. ______________________

____

c. ______________________

____

d. ______________________

____

e. ______________________

____

Exercise 21-2 (continued)

GENERAL JOURNAL PAGE ______

DATE		DESCRIPTION	POST. REF.	DEBIT	CREDIT

Exercise 21-3

GENERAL JOURNAL PAGE ______

DATE		DESCRIPTION	POST. REF.	DEBIT	CREDIT

Exercise 21-4

Name ____________________

Midtown Sportswear

Worksheet

Month Ended April 30, 20XX

ACCT. NO.	ACCOUNT NAME	TRIAL BALANCE		ADJUSTMENTS		ADJUSTED TRIAL BALANCE		INCOME STATEMENT		BALANCE SHEET	
		DEBIT	CREDIT	DEBIT	CREDIT	DEBIT	CREDIT	DEBIT	CREDIT	DEBIT	CREDIT
	Cash	5 000 00									
	Accounts Receivable	3 500 00									
	Allow. for Uncoll. Accts.				(f) 70 00						
	Merchandise Inventory	6 000 00		(b) 9 000 00	(a) 6 000 00						
	Supplies	500 00			(c) 200 00						
	Prepaid Insurance	1 200 00			(d) 100 00						
	Equipment	8 000 00									
	Acc. Depr. — Equipment				(e) 50 00						
	Accounts Payable		4 000 00								
	Deanna Weldon, Capital		17 700 00								
	Deanna Weldon, Withd.	800 00									
	Income Summary			(a) 6 000 00	(b) 9 000 00						
	Sales		19 000 00								
	Merchandise Purchases	10 000 00									
	Rent Expense	2 000 00									
	Salaries Expense	3 600 00									
	Supplies Expense			(c) 200 00							
	Insurance Expense			(d) 100 00							
	Depreciation Expense			(e) 50 00							
	Uncollectible Accts. Exp.			(f) 70 00							
	Miscellaneous Expense	100 00									
	Totals	40 700 00	40 700 00	15 420 00	15 420 00						

Problem 21-1

ACCT. NO.	ACCOUNT NAME	TRIAL BALANCE		ADJUSTMENTS		ADJUSTED TRIAL BALANCE		INCOME STATEMENT		BALANCE SHEET	
		DEBIT	CREDIT	DEBIT	CREDIT	DEBIT	CREDIT	DEBIT	CREDIT	DEBIT	CREDIT
	Carried Forward										

Problem 21-1 (continued)

Name ______________________________

ACCT. NO.	ACCOUNT NAME	TRIAL BALANCE		ADJUSTMENTS		ADJUSTED TRIAL BALANCE		INCOME STATEMENT		BALANCE SHEET	
		DEBIT	CREDIT	DEBIT	CREDIT	DEBIT	CREDIT	DEBIT	CREDIT	DEBIT	CREDIT
	Brought Forward										

See the self-check key at the back of this workbook.

Note: Save the worksheet for use in Problem 22-1 and 23-1.

Problem 21-2

ACCT. NO.	ACCOUNT NAME	TRIAL BALANCE		ADJUSTMENTS		ADJUSTED TRIAL BALANCE		INCOME STATEMENT		BALANCE SHEET	
		DEBIT	CREDIT	DEBIT	CREDIT	DEBIT	CREDIT	DEBIT	CREDIT	DEBIT	CREDIT
	Carried Forward										

Problem 21-2 (continued)

Name ______________________________

ACCT. NO.	ACCOUNT NAME	TRIAL BALANCE		ADJUSTMENTS		ADJUSTED TRIAL BALANCE		INCOME STATEMENT		BALANCE SHEET	
		DEBIT	CREDIT	DEBIT	CREDIT	DEBIT	CREDIT	DEBIT	CREDIT	DEBIT	CREDIT
	Brought Forward										

See the self-check key at the back of this workbook.

Note: Save the worksheet for use in Problem 22-2 and 23-2

Case Study 21

Name ______________________

Date ______________________

Chapter 22

COST OF GOODS SOLD AND STATEMENTS

Exercise 22-1

ACCT. NO.	ACCOUNT NAME	ADJUSTED TRIAL BALANCE DEBIT	ADJUSTED TRIAL BALANCE CREDIT	INCOME STATEMENT DEBIT	INCOME STATEMENT CREDIT	BALANCE SHEET DEBIT	BALANCE SHEET CREDIT
	Cash	8 000 00					
	Merchandise Inventory	8 000 00					
	Accounts Payable		5 000 00				
	Dave Fletcher, Capital		11 000 00				
	Dave Fletcher, Withdrawals	1 000 00					
	Income Summary	7 000 00	8 000 00				
	Sales		15 000 00				
	Merchandise Purchases	9 000 00					
	Selling Expenses	4 000 00					
	Office Expenses	2 000 00					
	Totals	39 000 00	39 000 00				

Exercise 22-2

Exercise 22-2 (continued)

Exercise 22-3

Name ______________________________

Exercise 22-4 (Complete the Worksheet on Page 199, Exercise 21-4)

Exercise 22-4 (continued)

Name

See the self-check key at the back of this workbook.

Problem 22-1

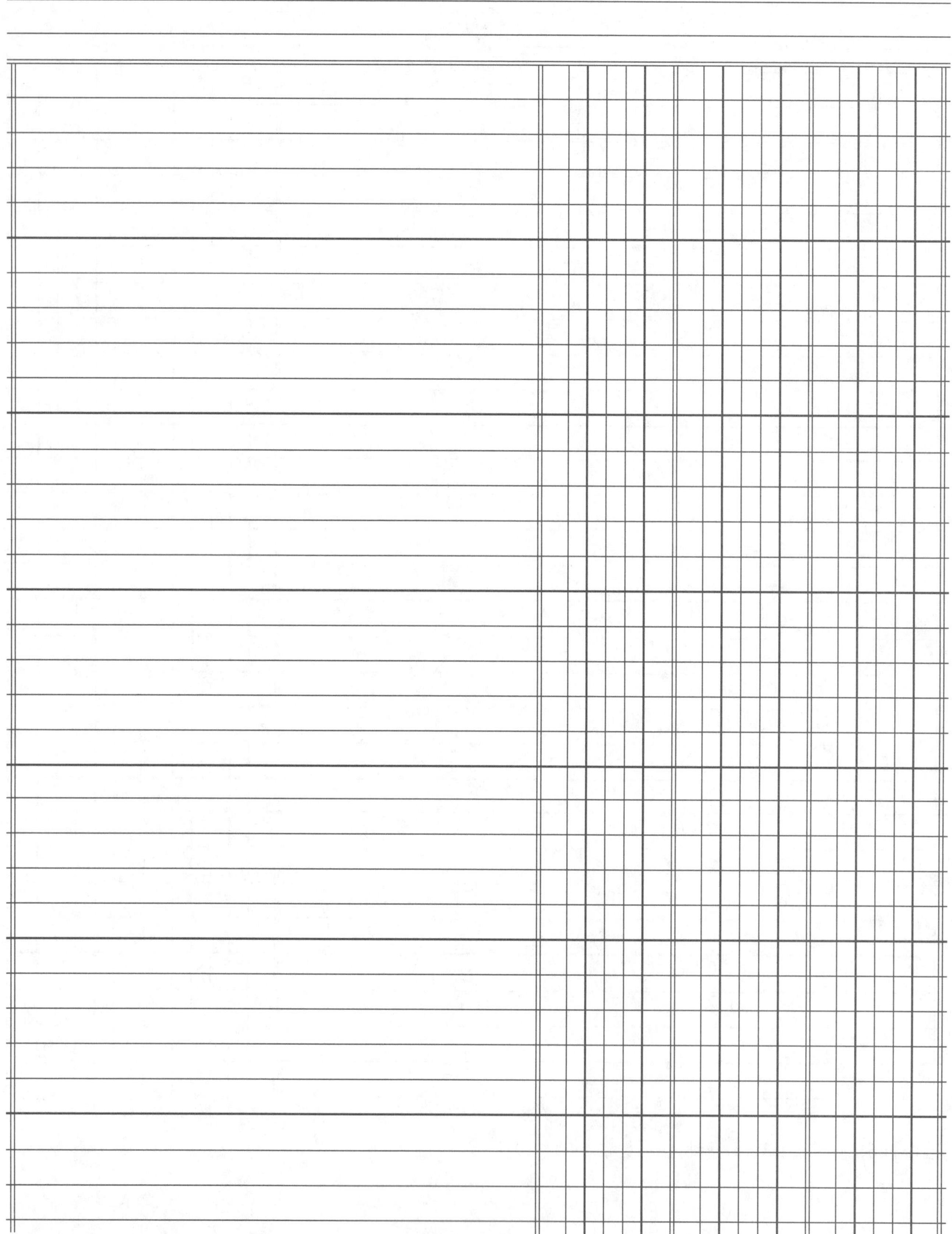

See the self-check key at the back of this workbook.

Name ______________________________

See the self-check key at the back of this workbook.

Problem 22-1 (continued)

See the self-check key at the back of this workbook.

Problem 22-2

Name ______________________________

See the self-check key at the back of this workbook.

Problem 22-2 (continued)

See the self-check key at the back of this workbook.

See the self-check key at the back of this workbook.

Problem 22-3

Name ____________________

Delmuth Wholesale Grocery Company

Worksheet

Month Ended March 31, 20XX

ACCT. NO.	ACCOUNT NAME	TRIAL BALANCE		ADJUSTMENTS		ADJUSTED TRIAL BALANCE		INCOME STATEMENT		BALANCE SHEET	
		DEBIT	CREDIT	DEBIT	CREDIT	DEBIT	CREDIT	DEBIT	CREDIT	DEBIT	CREDIT
101	Cash	3230 00									
112	Accounts Receivable	2500 00									
113	Allowance for										
	Uncollectible Accounts										
114	Merch. Inventory	9100 00									
115	Supplies	520 00									
116	Prepaid Insurance	600 00									
118	Delivery Equipment	6800 00									
119	Accum. Depr. —										
	Delivery Equipment		300 00								
120	Warehouse Equipment	3900 00									
121	Accum. Depr. —										
	Warehouse Equipment		90 00								
202	Accounts Payable		3200 00								
301	Kathryn Delmuth, Capital		19800 00								
399	Income Summary										
401	Sales		25570 00								
501	Merch. Purchases	20610 00									
511	Depr. Expense —										
	Delivery Equipment										
512	Depr. Expense —										
	Warehouse Equipment										
513	Insurance Expense										
514	Supplies Expense										
515	Truck Expense	110 00									
516	Wages Expense	1590 00									
517	Uncoll. Accts. Expense										
	Totals	48960 00	48960 00								
	Net Income										

See the self-check key at the back of this workbook.

Case Study 22

Chapter 23

Name ______________________

Date ______________________

ADJUSTING AND CLOSING THE GENERAL LEDGER

Exercise 23-1

GENERAL JOURNAL

PAGE ________

DATE	DESCRIPTION	POST. REF.	DEBIT	CREDIT

Exercise 23-2

GENERAL JOURNAL

PAGE ______

DATE		DESCRIPTION	POST. REF.	DEBIT	CREDIT

Exercise 23-3

GENERAL JOURNAL

PAGE ______

DATE		DESCRIPTION	POST. REF.	DEBIT	CREDIT

Exercise 23-3 (continued)

Name ______________________

Exercise 23-4

GENERAL JOURNAL

PAGE ________

DATE		DESCRIPTION	POST. REF.	DEBIT	CREDIT

Exercise 23-5

GENERAL JOURNAL

PAGE ________

DATE	DESCRIPTION	POST. REF.	DEBIT	CREDIT

Problem 23-1

Name ____________________

GENERAL JOURNAL

PAGE ________

DATE		DESCRIPTION	POST. REF.	DEBIT	CREDIT

Problem 23-1 (continued)

GENERAL JOURNAL

PAGE ________

DATE		DESCRIPTION	POST. REF.	DEBIT	CREDIT

See the self-check key at the back of this workbook.

Problem 23-2

Name ______________________

GENERAL JOURNAL

PAGE ________

DATE	DESCRIPTION	POST. REF.	DEBIT	CREDIT

Problem 23-2 (continued)

GENERAL JOURNAL PAGE ______

DATE		DESCRIPTION	POST. REF.	DEBIT	CREDIT

See the self-check key at the back of this workbook.

Problem 23-2 (continued)

Name ______________________

Cash — NO. 101

DATE		DESCRIPTION	POST REF.	DEBIT	CREDIT	BALANCE DEBIT	BALANCE CREDIT
20xx Dec.	31	Balance	✓			3,575.00	

Accounts Receivable — NO. 112

DATE		DESCRIPTION	POST REF.	DEBIT	CREDIT	BALANCE DEBIT	BALANCE CREDIT
20xx Dec.	31	Balance	✓			2,140.00	

Allowance for Uncollectible Accounts — NO. 113

DATE		DESCRIPTION	POST REF.	DEBIT	CREDIT	BALANCE DEBIT	BALANCE CREDIT

Merchandise Inventory — NO. 114

DATE		DESCRIPTION	POST REF.	DEBIT	CREDIT	BALANCE DEBIT	BALANCE CREDIT
20xx Dec.	31	Balance	✓			18,600.00	

Problem 23-2 (continued)

Supplies NO. 115

DATE		DESCRIPTION	POST REF.	DEBIT	CREDIT	BALANCE DEBIT	BALANCE CREDIT
20xx Dec.	31	Balance	✓			420 00	

Prepaid Insurance NO. 116

DATE		DESCRIPTION	POST REF.	DEBIT	CREDIT	BALANCE DEBIT	BALANCE CREDIT
20xx Dec.	31	Balance	✓			1440 00	

Office Equipment NO. 132

DATE		DESCRIPTION	POST REF.	DEBIT	CREDIT	BALANCE DEBIT	BALANCE CREDIT
20xx Dec.	31	Balance	✓			6960 00	

Accumulated Depreciation — Office Equipment NO. 133

DATE		DESCRIPTION	POST REF.	DEBIT	CREDIT	BALANCE DEBIT	BALANCE CREDIT
20xx Dec.	31	Balance	✓				360 00

Problem 23-2 (continued)

Name ______________________________

Warehouse Equipment NO. 134

DATE		DESCRIPTION	POST REF.	DEBIT	CREDIT	BALANCE DEBIT	BALANCE CREDIT
20xx Dec.	31	Balance	✓			16,000.00	

Accumulated Depreciation — Warehouse Equipment NO. 135

DATE		DESCRIPTION	POST REF.	DEBIT	CREDIT	BALANCE DEBIT	BALANCE CREDIT
20xx Dec.	31	Balance	✓				630.00

Accounts Payable NO. 202

DATE		DESCRIPTION	POST REF.	DEBIT	CREDIT	BALANCE DEBIT	BALANCE CREDIT
20xx Dec.	31	Balance	✓				1,760.00

Jeff Finsen, Capital NO. 301

DATE		DESCRIPTION	POST REF.	DEBIT	CREDIT	BALANCE DEBIT	BALANCE CREDIT
20xx Dec.	31	Balance	✓				45,325.00

Problem 23-2 (continued)

Jeff Finser, Withdrawals NO. 302

DATE		DESCRIPTION	POST REF.	DEBIT	CREDIT	BALANCE DEBIT	BALANCE CREDIT
20xx Dec.	31	Balance	✓			3 2 0 0 00	

Income Summary NO. 399

DATE		DESCRIPTION	POST REF.	DEBIT	CREDIT	BALANCE DEBIT	BALANCE CREDIT

Sales NO. 401

DATE		DESCRIPTION	POST REF.	DEBIT	CREDIT	BALANCE DEBIT	BALANCE CREDIT
20xx Dec.	31	Balance	✓				3 4 0 0 0 00

Sales Returns and Allowances NO. 402

DATE		DESCRIPTION	POST REF.	DEBIT	CREDIT	BALANCE DEBIT	BALANCE CREDIT
20xx Dec.	31	Balance	✓			5 6 0 00	

Problem 23-2 (continued)

Name ______________________

Sales Discount — NO. 403

DATE		DESCRIPTION	POST REF.	DEBIT	CREDIT	BALANCE DEBIT	BALANCE CREDIT
20xx Dec.	31	Balance	✓			620 00	

Merchandise Purchases — NO. 501

DATE		DESCRIPTION	POST REF.	DEBIT	CREDIT	BALANCE DEBIT	BALANCE CREDIT
20xx Dec.	31	Balance	✓			22500 00	

Freight In — NO. 502

DATE		DESCRIPTION	POST REF.	DEBIT	CREDIT	BALANCE DEBIT	BALANCE CREDIT
20xx Dec.	31	Balance	✓			430 00	

Purchases Returns and Allowances — NO. 503

DATE		DESCRIPTION	POST REF.	DEBIT	CREDIT	BALANCE DEBIT	BALANCE CREDIT
20xx Dec.	31	Balance	✓				485 00

Problem 23-2 (continued)

Purchases Discount NO. 504

DATE		DESCRIPTION	POST REF.	DEBIT	CREDIT	BALANCE DEBIT	BALANCE CREDIT
20xx Dec.	31	Balance	✓				225 00

Depreciation Expense — Office Equipment NO. 511

DATE		DESCRIPTION	POST REF.	DEBIT	CREDIT	BALANCE DEBIT	BALANCE CREDIT

Depreciation Expense — Warehouse Equipment NO. 512

DATE		DESCRIPTION	POST REF.	DEBIT	CREDIT	BALANCE DEBIT	BALANCE CREDIT

Rent Expense NO. 513

DATE		DESCRIPTION	POST REF.	DEBIT	CREDIT	BALANCE DEBIT	BALANCE CREDIT
20xx Dec.	31	Balance	✓			1950 00	

Problem 23-2 (continued)

Name ______________________

Supplies Expense NO. 514

DATE		DESCRIPTION	POST REF.	DEBIT	CREDIT	BALANCE DEBIT	BALANCE CREDIT

Wages Expense NO. 515

DATE		DESCRIPTION	POST REF.	DEBIT	CREDIT	BALANCE DEBIT	BALANCE CREDIT
20 Dec.	xx 31	Balance	✓			3,840.00	

Utilities Expense NO. 516

DATE		DESCRIPTION	POST REF.	DEBIT	CREDIT	BALANCE DEBIT	BALANCE CREDIT
20 Dec.	xx 31	Balance	✓			550.00	

Insurance Expense NO. 517

DATE		DESCRIPTION	POST REF.	DEBIT	CREDIT	BALANCE DEBIT	BALANCE CREDIT

Uncollectible Accounts Expense NO. 518

DATE		DESCRIPTION	POST REF.	DEBIT	CREDIT	BALANCE DEBIT	BALANCE CREDIT

Problem 23-2 (continued)

ACCT. NO.	ACCOUNT NAME	DEBIT	CREDIT

See the self-check key at the back of this workbook.

Case Study 23

Name ______________________________

Extra Form

GENERAL JOURNAL

PAGE ______

DATE		DESCRIPTION	POST. REF.	DEBIT	CREDIT

PROJECT 4

Name ______________________

Date ______________________

Note: The worksheet begins on the next page. Record the adjusting entries on the journal form below. Record the closing entries on the journal form following the worksheet. Post the adjusting and closing entries to the general ledger accounts that you prepared for Project 3.

GENERAL JOURNAL

PAGE ______

DATE		DESCRIPTION	POST. REF.	DEBIT	CREDIT

Project 4 (continued)

Leeser Lumber Company

Worksheet

Month Ended February 28, 20XX

	ACCT. NO.	ACCOUNT NAME	TRIAL BALANCE		ADJUSTMENTS	
			DEBIT	CREDIT	DEBIT	CREDIT
1	101	Cash				
2	112	Accounts Receivable				
3	113	Allow. for Uncoll. Accts.				
4	114	Merch. Inventory				
5	115	Supplies				
6	116	Prepaid Insurance				
7	126	Office Equipment				
8	127	Acc. Depr. — Off. Equip.				
9	128	Warehouse Equipment				
10	129	Acc. Depr. — Ware. Equip.				
11	202	Accounts Payable				
12	231	Sales Tax Payable				
13	301	Anthony Leeser, Capital				
14	302	Anthony Leeser, Withdrawals				
15	399	Income Summary				
16	401	Sales				
17	402	Sales Ret. & Allow.				
18	403	Sales Discount				
19	501	Merch. Purchases				
20	502	Freight In				
21	503	Purchases Ret. & Allow.				
22	504	Purchases Discount				
23	511	Advertising Expense				
24	512	Telephone Expense				
25	513	Depr. Exp. — Off. Equip.				
26	514	Depr. Exp. — Ware. Equip.				
27	515	Rent Expense				
28	517	Supplies Expense				
29	518	Utilities Expense				
30	519	Wages Expense				
31	520	Uncoll. Acct. Exp.				
32	521	Insurance Expense				
33		Totals				
34		Net Income				
35						

See the self-check key at the back of this workbook.

Project 4 (continued)

Name ______________________________

ADJUSTED TRIAL BALANCE		INCOME STATEMENT		BALANCE SHEET		
DEBIT	CREDIT	DEBIT	CREDIT	DEBIT	CREDIT	
						1
						2
						3
						4
						5
						6
						7
						8
						9
						10
						11
						12
						13
						14
						15
						16
						17
						18
						19
						20
						21
						22
						23
						24
						25
						26
						27
						28
						29
						30
						31
						32
						33
						34
						35

See the self-check key at the back of this workbook.

Project 4 (continued)

GENERAL JOURNAL

PAGE ________

DATE		DESCRIPTION	POST. REF.	DEBIT	CREDIT

See the self-check key at the back of this workbook.

Project 4 (continued)

Name ____________________

See the self-check key at the back of this workbook.

Project 4 (continued)

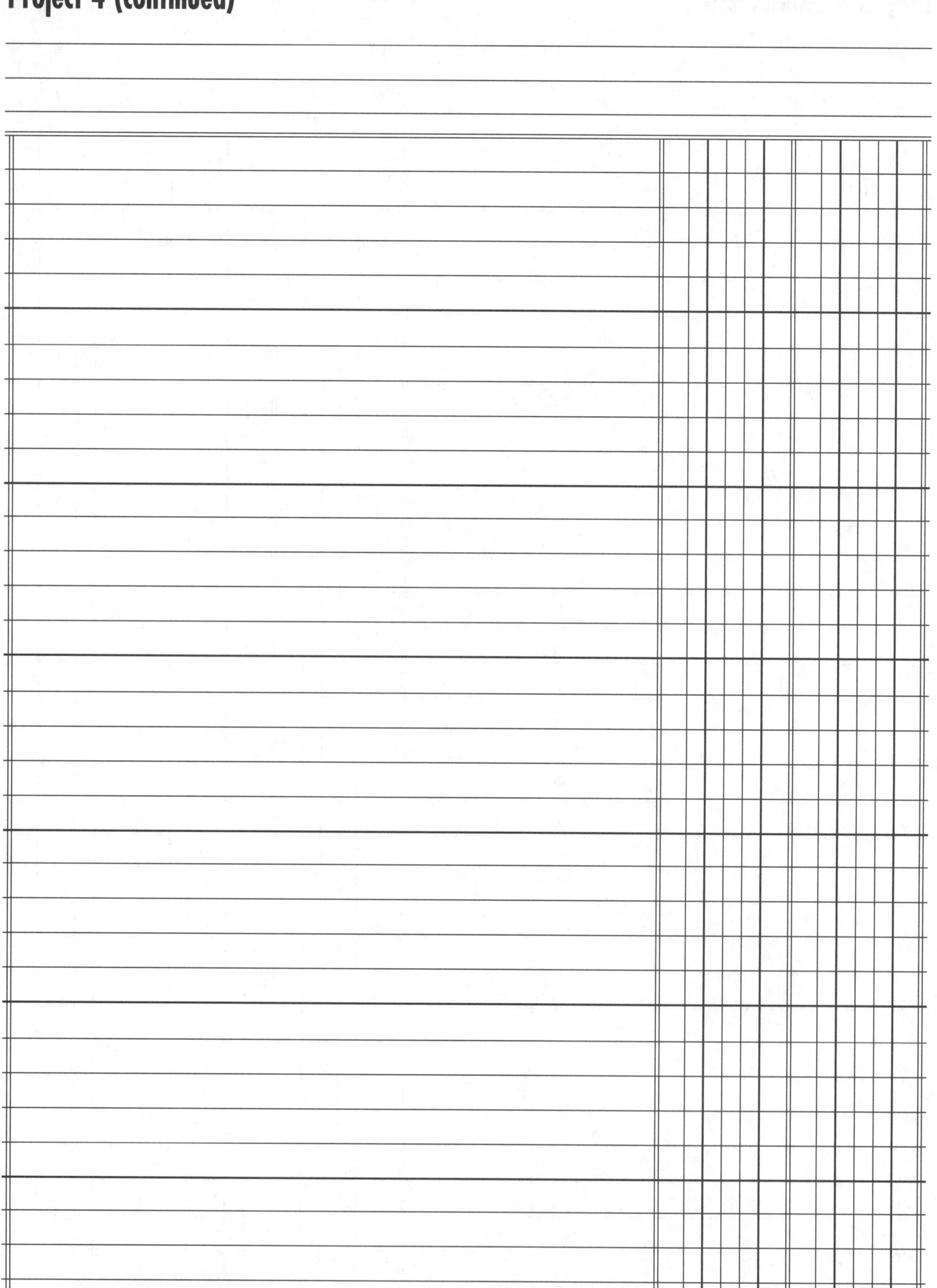

See the self-check key at the back of this workbook.

Project 4 (continued)

Name ____________________________

See the self-check key at the back of this workbook.

Project 4 (continued)

ACCT. NO.	ACCOUNT NAME	DEBIT	CREDIT

See the self-check key at the back of this workbook.

Chapter 24

Name ____________________

Date ____________________

BANKING PROCEDURES

Exercise 24-1

THIS FORM IS PROVIDED TO HELP YOU RECONCILE YOUR BANK STATEMENT

______________________ 20 ____

BALANCE SHOWN ON BANK STATEMENT $ ________

Add: Deposits Not on Statement

Date	Amount		
Total			$

SUBTOTAL $ ________

Subtract: Checks Issued But Not on Statement

Number	Amount		
Total			$

ADJUSTED BANK BALANCE $ ________

BALANCE SHOWN IN CHECKBOOK $ ________

Add: Corrections

Description	Amount		
Total			$

SUBTOTAL $ ________

Subtract: Bank Charges Not in Checkbook and Corrections

Description	Amount		
Service Charge			
Total			$

ADJUSTED CHECKBOOK BALANCE $ ________

Exercise 24-2

THIS FORM IS PROVIDED TO HELP YOU RECONCILE YOUR BANK STATEMENT

______________________ 20 ____

BALANCE SHOWN ON BANK STATEMENT $ ________

Add: Deposits Not on Statement

Date	Amount	
Total		$

SUBTOTAL $ ________

Subtract: Checks Issued But Not on Statement

Number	Amount	
Total		$

ADJUSTED BANK BALANCE $ ________

BALANCE SHOWN IN CHECKBOOK $ ________

Add: Corrections

Description	Amount	
Total		$

SUBTOTAL $ ________

Subtract: Bank Charges Not in Checkbook and Corrections

Description	Amount	
Service Charge		
Total		$

ADJUSTED CHECKBOOK BALANCE $ ________

Exercise 24-3

THIS FORM IS PROVIDED TO HELP YOU RECONCILE YOUR BANK STATEMENT

______________________ 20 ____

BALANCE SHOWN ON BANK STATEMENT $ ________

Add: Deposits Not on Statement

Date	Amount	
Total		$

SUBTOTAL $ ________

Subtract: Checks Issued But Not on Statement

Number	Amount	
Total		$

ADJUSTED BANK BALANCE $ ________

BALANCE SHOWN IN CHECKBOOK $ ________

Add: Corrections

Description	Amount	
Total		$

SUBTOTAL $ ________

Subtract: Bank Charges Not in Checkbook and Corrections

Description	Amount	
Service Charge		
Total		$

ADJUSTED CHECKBOOK BALANCE $ ________

Problem 24-1

Name ______________________________

Blank Endorsement

Full Endorsement

Restrictive Endorsement

Deposited in

MOUNTAIN NATIONAL BANK
Fort Collins, Colorado 80521

Date ______________________________

Deposit to
Account of

MIGUEL'S MUSIC CENTER
1272 WEST FAIRFAX STREET
FORT COLLINS, COLORADO 80521

⑆0⑆⑈9⑆9⑈

	Dollars	Cents
Currency		
Coin		
Checks 1		
(List separately) 2		
3		
4		
5		
6		
7		
TOTAL		

This deposit accepted under and subject to the provisions of the Uniform Commercial Code

See the self-check key at the back of this workbook.

Problem 24-2

Note: Use this check stub to record the deposit computed in Problem 24-1.

NO. ________ $ ________
DATE ________
TO ________
FOR ________

	DOLLARS	CENTS
BALANCE	4,152	10
AMT. DEPOSITED		
TOTAL		
AMT. THIS CHECK		
BALANCE		

MIGUEL'S MUSIC CENTER
1272 WEST FAIRFAX STREET
FORT COLLINS, COLORADO 80521

NO. ________

82-25
1021

PAY TO THE ORDER OF ________ 20____ $ ________

________ DOLLARS

MOUNTAIN NATIONAL BANK
Fort Collins, Colorado 80521

⑆1021⑈0025⑆ 401⑈919⑈

See the self-check key at the back of this workbook.

Problem 24-3

THIS FORM IS PROVIDED TO HELP YOU RECONCILE YOUR BANK STATEMENT

________ 20 ____

BALANCE SHOWN ON BANK STATEMENT $ ________

Add: Deposits Not on Statement

Date	Amount	
Total		$

SUBTOTAL $ ________

Subtract: Checks Issued But Not on Statement

Number	Amount	
Total		$

ADJUSTED BANK BALANCE $ ________

BALANCE SHOWN IN CHECKBOOK $ ________

Add: Corrections

Description	Amount	
Total		$

SUBTOTAL $ ________

Subtract: Bank Charges Not in Checkbook and Corrections

Description	Amount	
Service Charge		
Total		$

ADJUSTED CHECKBOOK BALANCE $ ________

See the self-check key at the back of this workbook.

Name ______________________

GENERAL JOURNAL

PAGE ________

DATE		DESCRIPTION	POST. REF.	DEBIT	CREDIT

Problem 24-4

Note: Use the form on the next page for the bank reconciliation.

GENERAL JOURNAL

PAGE ________

DATE		DESCRIPTION	POST. REF.	DEBIT	CREDIT

Problem 24-4 (continued)

Elmer E. Mears, M.D.

Bank Reconciliation

May 2, 20XX

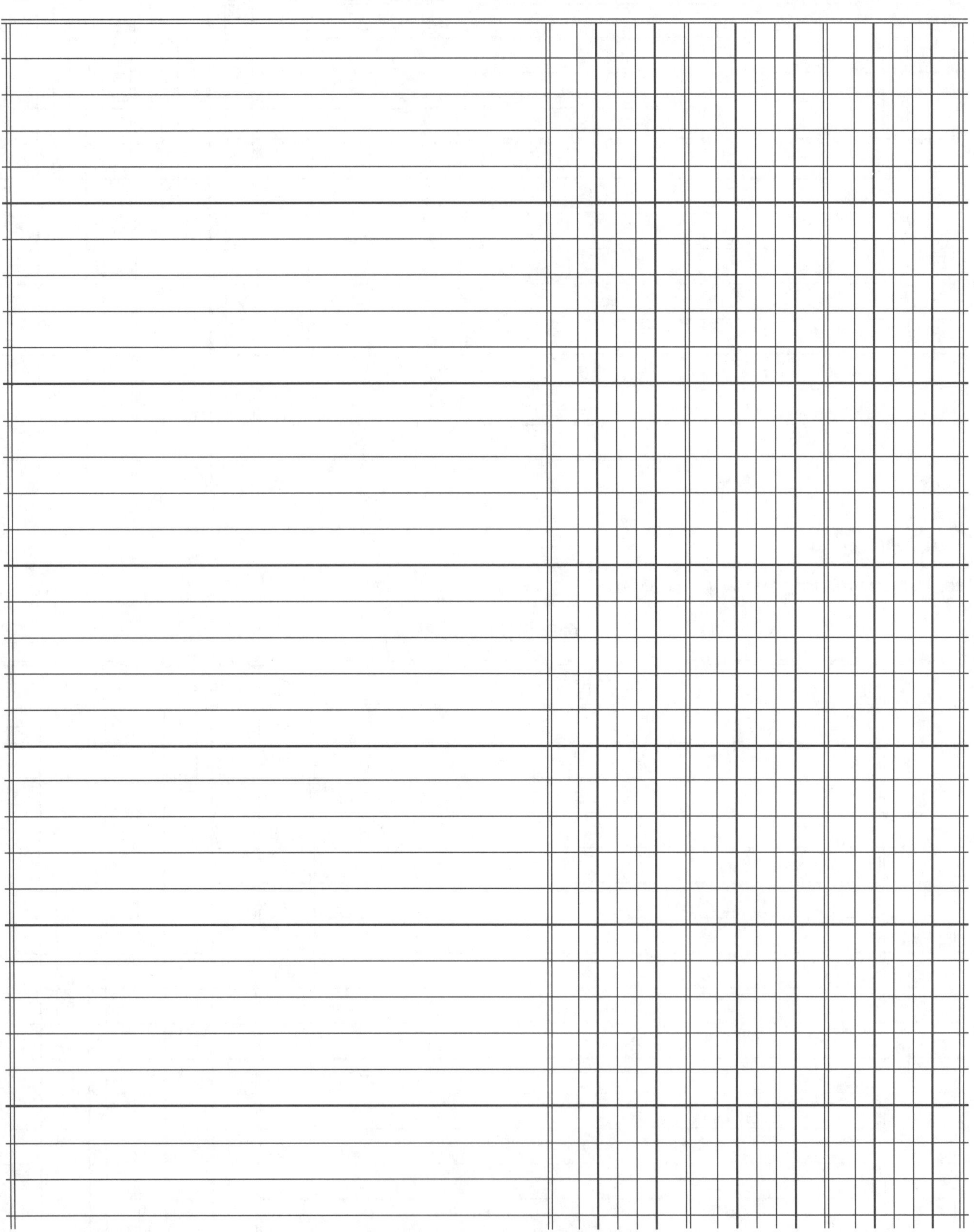

See the self-check key at the back of this workbook.

Case Study 24

Name ______________________________

Extra Form

THIS FORM IS PROVIDED TO HELP YOU RECONCILE YOUR BANK STATEMENT

______________________ 20 ____

BALANCE SHOWN ON BANK STATEMENT $ ________

Add: Deposits Not on Statement

Date	Amount	
Total		$

SUBTOTAL $ ________

Subtract: Checks Issued
But Not on Statement

Number	Amount	
Total		$

ADJUSTED BANK BALANCE $ ________

BALANCE SHOWN IN CHECKBOOK $ ________

Add: Corrections

Description	Amount	
Total		$

SUBTOTAL $ ________

Subtract: Bank Charges
Not in Checkbook and Corrections

Description	Amount	
Service Charge		
Total		$

ADJUSTED CHECKBOOK BALANCE $ ________

Chapter 25

Name

Date

PETTY CASH AND OTHER SPECIAL CASH PROCEDURES

Exercise 25-1

ACCT. NO.	ACCOUNT NAME	DEBIT	CREDIT

Exercise 25-2

ACCT. NO.	ACCOUNT NAME	DEBIT	CREDIT

Name ______________________

Proof of Petty Cash Fund
June 30, 20XX

See the self-check key at the back of this workbook.

Problem 25-1 (continued)

CASH PAYMENTS JOURNAL for Month of ______ 20 ___ PAGE ___

DATE	CHECK NO.	EXPLANATION	ACCOUNTS PAYABLE		MERCHANDISE PURCHASES DEBIT	OTHER ACCOUNTS DEBIT			PUCHASES DISCOUNT CREDIT	CASH CREDIT
			✓	DEBIT		ACCOUNT NAME	POST REF.	AMOUNT		

Name ______________________

Request for Replenishment of Petty Cash Fund
June 30, 20XX

See the self-check key at the back of this workbook.

Problem 25-2

CASH RECEIPTS JOURNAL for Month of ______________ 20 ____ PAGE ____

DATE		EXPLANATION	ACCOUNTS RECEIVABLE		SALES TAX PAYABLE CREDIT	SALES CREDIT	OTHER ACCOUNTS DEBIT			SALES DISCOUNT DEBIT	CASH DEBIT
			✓	CREDIT			ACCOUNT NAME	POST REF.	AMOUNT		

See the self-check key at the back of this workbook.

Case Study 25

Name ______________________

Extra Form

CASH RECEIPTS JOURNAL for Month of ______________ 20 ____ PAGE ____

DATE	EXPLANATION	ACCOUNTS RECEIVABLE		SALES TAX PAYABLE CREDIT	SALES CREDIT	OTHER ACCOUNTS CREDIT			SALES DISCOUNT DEBIT	CASH DEBIT
		✓	CREDIT			ACCOUNT NAME	POST REF.	AMOUNT		

Chapter 26

Name ______________________________

Date ______________________________

PAYROLL RECORDS

Exercise 26-1

	Pay Period				
	Yearly	Monthly	Semimonthly	Biweekly	Weekly
Example	$16,224	$1,352	$676	$624	$312
1					
2					
3					
4					
Totals					

Exercise 26-2

Employee	Rate Per Hour	Hours			Earnings		
		Total	Regular	Overtime	Regular	Overtime	Gross
M. Carr	$8.00	46					
N. Diaz	10.50	42					
S. Evans	9.80	44					
L. Sklar	10.30	45					

Exercise 26-3

Employee	Units Produced					Total Units	Gross Earnings
	Mon.	Tue.	Wed.	Thur.	Fri.		
J. Olson	140	145	149	138	150		
S. McNair	150	155	151	140	153		
V. Ruiz	151	149	156	158	155		
C. Russo	146	148	147	145	149		

Exercise 26-4

Employee	Daily Sales						Total Sales	Gross Earnings
	Mon.	Tue.	Wed.	Thur.	Fri.	Sat.		
S. Cohen	$650	$520		$830	$490	$810		
M. Jackson	540		370	610	905	750		
W. Klein		752	694	547	625	807		
J. Rivera	625	575		952	639	825		

Exercise 26-5

Employee	Total Sales	Salary	Commission	Gross Earnings
L. Alexander				
R. Diaz				
J. Kominski				
A. Sullivan				

Exercise 26-6

Employee	With. Allow.	Mar. St.	Gross Earnings	Income Tax	Soc. Sec.	Medi-care	Total Deductions	Net Pay
J. Alvarez	1	S	$445					
L. Levine	2	M	540					
R. Summers	3	M	565					
W. Toler	4	M	460					

GENERAL JOURNAL PAGE ____

DATE		DESCRIPTION	POST. REF.	DEBIT	CREDIT

Exercise 26-7

GENERAL JOURNAL PAGE ____

DATE		DESCRIPTION	POST. REF.	DEBIT	CREDIT

Exercise 26-8

Name ______________________________

GENERAL JOURNAL

PAGE ________

DATE		DESCRIPTION	POST. REF.	DEBIT	CREDIT

Exercise 26-9

GENERAL JOURNAL

PAGE ________

DATE		DESCRIPTION	POST. REF.	DEBIT	CREDIT

Problem 26-1

NO. 1 NAME Heather DeCosta

WITHHOLDING ALLOWANCES 1 MARITAL STATUS S

WEEK ENDING June 30, 20XX

DEDUCTIONS	
Fed. Income Tax	GROSS EARNINGS
Social Security Tax	LESS TOTAL DEDUCTIONS
Medicare Tax	NET PAY
Medical Insurance	
Savings Bonds	
TOTAL DEDUCTIONS	

Days	MORNING		AFTERNOON		EVENING		Daily Tot.
	IN	OUT	IN	OUT	IN	OUT	
Sa							
Su							
M	7:56	12:01	1:00	5:01	6:00	8:00	
Tu	7:58	12:00	12:58	5:03			
W	7:55	12:01	12:59	5:02			
Th	8:01	12:00	1:00	6:00			
F	7:57	11:59	12:59	5:03	6:00	8:01	

		HOURS	RATE	EARNINGS
	REGULAR		$8.00	
	OVERTIME		12.00	
DAYS WORKED	TOTAL HOURS		GROSS EARNINGS	

See the self-check key at the back of this workbook.

Problem 26-2

Name ______________________

PAYROLL REGISTER

WEEK BEGINNING ____________ 20 ___ AND ENDING ____________ 20 ___ PAID ____________ 20 ___

EMP. NO.	NAME	WITH. ALLOW.	MARITAL STATUS	HOURS WORKED		REG. HRLY. RATE	OVER-TIME RATE	EARNINGS			DEDUCTIONS				NET PAY	
				REG.	OVER-TIME			REGULAR	OT.	TOTAL	INCOME TAX	SOC. SEC.	MEDI-CARE	TOTAL	AMOUNT	CK. NO.

See the self-check key at the back of this workbook.

Problem 26-3

GENERAL JOURNAL PAGE ______

DATE		DESCRIPTION	POST. REF.	DEBIT	CREDIT

See the self-check key at the back of this workbook.

Problem 26-4

Name ____________________

CASH PAYMENTS JOURNAL for Month of ____________________ 20 ____ PAGE ____

DATE	CHECK NO.	EXPLANATION	ACCOUNTS PAYABLE		MERCHANDISE PURCHASES DEBIT	OTHER ACCOUNTS DEBIT			PUCHASES DISCOUNT CREDIT	CASH CREDIT
			✓	DEBIT		ACCOUNT NAME	POST REF.	AMOUNT		

Case Study 26

Chapter 27

Name ______________________

Date ______________________

THE COMBINED JOURNAL

Exercise 27-1

Ex.	Debit	Credit		Debit	Credit
Ex.	*i*	*b*			
1.	______	______	6.	______	______
2.	______	______	7.	______	______
3.	______	______	8.	______	______
4.	______	______	9.	______	______
5.	______	______	10.	______	______

Exercise 27-2

COMBINED JOURNAL for Month of ______________________ 20 ______ PAGE ______

	DATE	CK. NO.	CASH		OTHER ACCOUNTS				
			DEBIT	CREDIT	ACCOUNT NAME	POST REF.	DEBIT AMOUNT	CREDIT AMOUNT	
1									1
2									2
3									3
4									4
5									5
6									6
7									7
8									8
9									9
10									10
11									11
12									12
13									13
14									14
15									15
16									16
17									17
18									18
19									19
20									20

Problem 27-1

COMBINED JOURNAL for Month of ______________ 20 ____

	DATE	CK. NO.	EXPLANATION	CASH		ACCOUNTS RECEIVABLE		
				DEBIT	CREDIT	✓	DEBIT	CREDIT
1								
2								
3								
4								
5								
6								
7								
8								
9								
10								
11								
12								
13								
14								
15								
16								
17								
18								
19								
20								
21								
22								
23								
24								
25								
26								
27								
28								
29								
30								
31								
32								
33								
34								
35								

See the self-check key at the back of this workbook.

Problem 27-1 (continued)

Name ______________________

PAGE ______

ACCOUNTS PAYABLE			MERCH. PURCHASES DEBIT	SALES CREDIT	OTHER ACCOUNTS			
✓	DEBIT	CREDIT			ACCOUNT NAME	POST REF.	DEBIT AMOUNT	CREDIT AMOUNT

Problem 27-1 (continued)

ACCT. NO.	ACCOUNT NAME	DEBIT	CREDIT

See the self-check key at the back of this workbook.

Case Study 27

Name ______________________________

Extra Form

ACCT. NO.	ACCOUNT NAME	DEBIT	CREDIT

PRACTICE SET

Name ____________________

Date ____________________

GENERAL JOURNAL

PAGE 17

DATE		DESCRIPTION	POST. REF.	DEBIT	CREDIT

Practice Set (continued)

GENERAL JOURNAL

PAGE 18

DATE		DESCRIPTION	POST. REF.	DEBIT	CREDIT

Name ______________________________

GENERAL JOURNAL

PAGE 19

DATE		DESCRIPTION	POST. REF.	DEBIT	CREDIT

Practice Set (continued)

GENERAL JOURNAL

PAGE 20

DATE		DESCRIPTION	POST. REF.	DEBIT	CREDIT

Practice Set (continued)

Name ______________________

SALES JOURNAL for Month of May 20 XX PAGE 5

DATE		INV. NO.	CUSTOMER'S ACCOUNT	ACCOUNTS RECEIVABLE ✓	ACCOUNTS RECEIVABLE DEBIT	SALES TAX PAYABLE CREDIT	SALES CREDIT

See the self-check key at the back of this workbook.

PURCHASES JOURNAL for Month of May 20 XX PAGE 5

DATE		CREDITOR'S ACCOUNT CREDITED	POST REF.	INVOICE NUMBER	INV. DATE	TERMS	ACCOUNTS PAYABLE CREDIT	MERCH. PURCHASES DEBIT	FREIGHT IN DEBIT

See the self-check key at the back of this workbook.

CASH RECEIPTS JOURNAL for Month of MAY 20 XX PAGE 5

DATE	EXPLANATION	ACCOUNTS RECEIVABLE ✓	ACCOUNTS RECEIVABLE CREDIT	SALES TAX PAYABLE CREDIT	SALES CREDIT	OTHER ACCOUNTS CREDIT ACCOUNT NAME	OTHER ACCOUNTS CREDIT POST REF.	OTHER ACCOUNTS CREDIT AMOUNT	SALES DISCOUNT DEBIT	CASH DEBIT

See the self-check key at the back of this workbook.

Name ______________________

CASH PAYMENTS JOURNAL for Month of MAY 20 XX PAGE 10

DATE	CHECK NO.	EXPLANATION	ACCOUNTS PAYABLE		MERCHANDISE PURCHASES DEBIT	OTHER ACCOUNTS DEBIT			PURCHASES DISCOUNT CREDIT	CASH CREDIT
			✓	DEBIT		ACCOUNT NAME	POST REF.	AMOUNT		
		Carried Forward								

Note: When you reach the last line of this form, add the amount in each column, and bring the totals forward to the next page. Then you can continue recording cash payments for the month.

CASH PAYMENTS JOURNAL for Month of MAY 20 XX PAGE 11

DATE	CHECK NO.	EXPLANATION	ACCOUNTS PAYABLE		MERCHANDISE PURCHASES DEBIT	OTHER ACCOUNTS DEBIT			PURCHASES DISCOUNT CREDIT	CASH CREDIT
			✓	DEBIT		ACCOUNT NAME	POST REF.	AMOUNT		
		Brought Forward								

See the self-check key at the back of this workbook.

Practice Set (continued)

Name ______________________

Cash NO. 101

DATE		DESCRIPTION	POST REF.	DEBIT	CREDIT	BALANCE DEBIT	BALANCE CREDIT
20XX May	1	Balance	✓			41,360.84	

Petty Cash NO. 102

DATE		DESCRIPTION	POST REF.	DEBIT	CREDIT	BALANCE DEBIT	BALANCE CREDIT
20XX May	1	Balance	✓			50.00	

Notes Receivable NO. 111

DATE		DESCRIPTION	POST REF.	DEBIT	CREDIT	BALANCE DEBIT	BALANCE CREDIT

Accounts Receivable NO. 112

DATE		DESCRIPTION	POST REF.	DEBIT	CREDIT	BALANCE DEBIT	BALANCE CREDIT
20XX May	1	Balance	✓			6,324.00	

Practice Set (continued)

Allowance for Uncollectible Accounts NO. 113

DATE		DESCRIPTION	POST REF.	DEBIT	CREDIT	BALANCE DEBIT	BALANCE CREDIT

Merchandise Inventory NO. 114

DATE		DESCRIPTION	POST REF.	DEBIT	CREDIT	BALANCE DEBIT	BALANCE CREDIT
20XX May	1	Balance	✓			543,182.6	

Supplies NO. 115

DATE		DESCRIPTION	POST REF.	DEBIT	CREDIT	BALANCE DEBIT	BALANCE CREDIT
20XX May	1	Balance	✓			3,182.41	

Prepaid Insurance NO. 116

DATE		DESCRIPTION	POST REF.	DEBIT	CREDIT	BALANCE DEBIT	BALANCE CREDIT

Store Equipment NO. 121

DATE		DESCRIPTION	POST REF.	DEBIT	CREDIT	BALANCE DEBIT	BALANCE CREDIT
20XX May	1	Balance	✓			26,450.00	

Practice Set (continued)

Name ____________________

Accumulated Depreciation — Store Equipment NO. 122

DATE		DESCRIPTION	POST REF.	DEBIT	CREDIT	BALANCE DEBIT	BALANCE CREDIT
20XX May	1	Balance	✓				7200 00

Office Equipment NO. 123

DATE		DESCRIPTION	POST REF.	DEBIT	CREDIT	BALANCE DEBIT	BALANCE CREDIT
20XX May	1	Balance	✓			45000 00	

Accumulated Depreciation — Office Equipment NO. 124

DATE		DESCRIPTION	POST REF.	DEBIT	CREDIT	BALANCE DEBIT	BALANCE CREDIT
20XX May	1	Balance	✓				12600 00

Notes Payable NO. 201

DATE		DESCRIPTION	POST REF.	DEBIT	CREDIT	BALANCE DEBIT	BALANCE CREDIT

Accounts Payable NO. 202

DATE		DESCRIPTION	POST REF.	DEBIT	CREDIT	BALANCE DEBIT	BALANCE CREDIT
20XX May	1	Balance	✓				8287 00

Practice Set (continued)

Employee Income Tax Payable — NO. 221

DATE		DESCRIPTION	POST REF.	DEBIT	CREDIT	BALANCE DEBIT	BALANCE CREDIT
20XX May	1	Balance	✓				874 00

Social Security Tax Payable — NO. 222

DATE		DESCRIPTION	POST REF.	DEBIT	CREDIT	BALANCE DEBIT	BALANCE CREDIT
20XX May	1	Balance	✓				1,518 76

Medicare Tax Payable — NO. 223

DATE		DESCRIPTION	POST REF.	DEBIT	CREDIT	BALANCE DEBIT	BALANCE CREDIT
20XX May	1	Balance	✓				355 20

Federal Unemployment Tax Payable — NO. 224

DATE		DESCRIPTION	POST REF.	DEBIT	CREDIT	BALANCE DEBIT	BALANCE CREDIT
20XX May	1	Balance	✓				97 98

Practice Set (continued)

Name ______________________

State Unemployment Tax Payable — NO. 225

DATE		DESCRIPTION	POST REF.	DEBIT	CREDIT	BALANCE DEBIT	BALANCE CREDIT
20XX May	1	Balance	✓				575 66

Salaries Payable — NO. 226

DATE		DESCRIPTION	POST REF.	DEBIT	CREDIT	BALANCE DEBIT	BALANCE CREDIT

Sales Tax Payable — NO. 231

DATE		DESCRIPTION	POST REF.	DEBIT	CREDIT	BALANCE DEBIT	BALANCE CREDIT
20XX May	1	Balance	✓				3,221 36

Tricia Brennan, Capital — NO. 301

DATE		DESCRIPTION	POST REF.	DEBIT	CREDIT	BALANCE DEBIT	BALANCE CREDIT
20XX May	1	Balance	✓				141,955 55

Tricia Brennan, Withdrawals — NO. 302

DATE		DESCRIPTION	POST REF.	DEBIT	CREDIT	BALANCE DEBIT	BALANCE CREDIT

Practice Set (continued)

Income Summary NO. 399

DATE		DESCRIPTION	POST REF.	DEBIT	CREDIT	BALANCE DEBIT	BALANCE CREDIT

Sales NO. 401

DATE		DESCRIPTION	POST REF.	DEBIT	CREDIT	BALANCE DEBIT	BALANCE CREDIT

Sales Returns and Allowances NO. 402

DATE		DESCRIPTION	POST REF.	DEBIT	CREDIT	BALANCE DEBIT	BALANCE CREDIT

Sales Discount NO. 403

DATE		DESCRIPTION	POST REF.	DEBIT	CREDIT	BALANCE DEBIT	BALANCE CREDIT

Interest Income NO. 491

DATE		DESCRIPTION	POST REF.	DEBIT	CREDIT	BALANCE DEBIT	BALANCE CREDIT

Merchandise Purchases NO. 501

DATE		DESCRIPTION	POST REF.	DEBIT	CREDIT	BALANCE DEBIT	BALANCE CREDIT

Practice Set (continued)

Name ______________________

Freight In NO. 502

DATE		DESCRIPTION	POST REF.	DEBIT	CREDIT	BALANCE	
						DEBIT	CREDIT

Purchases Returns and Allowances NO. 503

DATE		DESCRIPTION	POST REF.	DEBIT	CREDIT	BALANCE	
						DEBIT	CREDIT

Purchases Discount NO. 504

DATE		DESCRIPTION	POST REF.	DEBIT	CREDIT	BALANCE	
						DEBIT	CREDIT

Advertising Expense NO. 511

DATE		DESCRIPTION	POST REF.	DEBIT	CREDIT	BALANCE	
						DEBIT	CREDIT

Telephone Expense NO. 512

DATE		DESCRIPTION	POST REF.	DEBIT	CREDIT	BALANCE	
						DEBIT	CREDIT

Practice Set (continued)

Depreciation Expense — Store Equipment NO. 513

DATE	DESCRIPTION	POST REF.	DEBIT	CREDIT	BALANCE	
					DEBIT	CREDIT

Depreciation Expense — Office Equipment NO. 514

DATE	DESCRIPTION	POST REF.	DEBIT	CREDIT	BALANCE	
					DEBIT	CREDIT

Payroll Taxes Expense NO. 516

DATE	DESCRIPTION	POST REF.	DEBIT	CREDIT	BALANCE	
					DEBIT	CREDIT

Rent Expense NO. 517

DATE	DESCRIPTION	POST REF.	DEBIT	CREDIT	BALANCE	
					DEBIT	CREDIT

Supplies Expense NO. 518

DATE	DESCRIPTION	POST REF.	DEBIT	CREDIT	BALANCE	
					DEBIT	CREDIT

Utilities Expense NO. 519

DATE	DESCRIPTION	POST REF.	DEBIT	CREDIT	BALANCE	
					DEBIT	CREDIT

Practice Set (continued)

Name ______________________

Salaries Expense NO. 520

DATE		DESCRIPTION	POST REF.	DEBIT	CREDIT	BALANCE	
						DEBIT	CREDIT

Uncollectible Accounts Expense NO. 521

DATE		DESCRIPTION	POST REF.	DEBIT	CREDIT	BALANCE	
						DEBIT	CREDIT

Insurance Expense NO. 522

DATE		DESCRIPTION	POST REF.	DEBIT	CREDIT	BALANCE	
						DEBIT	CREDIT

Miscellaneous Expense NO. 536

DATE		DESCRIPTION	POST REF.	DEBIT	CREDIT	BALANCE	
						DEBIT	CREDIT

Practice Set (continued)

ACCOUNTS RECEIVABLE LEDGER

NAME Botzer Builders
ADDRESS Gold Club Drive
Langhome, PA 19047
TERMS: 1/10, n/30

DATE		DESCRIPTION	POST. REF.	DEBIT	CREDIT	BALANCE

NAME Duld Lighting
ADDRESS 1441 Signpost Road
Richboro, PA 18954
TERMS: 1/10, n/30

DATE		DESCRIPTION	POST. REF.	DEBIT	CREDIT	BALANCE
20XX May	1	Balance	✓			3750 00

NAME Illuminations
ADDRESS 751 Venus Drive
Mt. Laurel, NJ 21567
TERMS: 1/10, n/30

DATE		DESCRIPTION	POST. REF.	DEBIT	CREDIT	BALANCE

Name ______________________

NAME Fagan Contractors
ADDRESS 732 Central Avenue
Rahway, NJ 07065
TERMS: 1/10, n/30

DATE		DESCRIPTION	POST. REF.	DEBIT	CREDIT	BALANCE

NAME Leidy and Gabriel
ADDRESS RR2, Box 1124
Mifflintown, PA 17059
TERMS: 1/10, n/30

DATE		DESCRIPTION	POST. REF.	DEBIT	CREDIT	BALANCE
20	XX					
May	1	Balance	✓			2 5 7 4 00

ACCOUNTS PAYABLE LEDGER

NAME Ruth Ann's Service
ADDRESS 45 Main Street
Doylestown, PA 18901
TERMS: n/30

DATE		DESCRIPTION	POST. REF.	DEBIT	CREDIT	BALANCE
20	XX					
May	1	Balance	✓			3 2 5 00

NAME Baskets by Pat
ADDRESS 831 Weaving Way
Tyler, PA 18948
TERMS: 2/10, n/30

DATE		DESCRIPTION	POST. REF.	DEBIT	CREDIT	BALANCE

NAME Gardzinski Electric
ADDRESS 1212 Brown Bark Road
Fairless Hills, PA 19030
TERMS: 1/15, n/30

DATE		DESCRIPTION	POST. REF.	DEBIT	CREDIT	BALANCE

Practice Set (continued)

NAME Grady Electric
ADDRESS 1414 South State Street
Newtown, PA 18940

TERMS: 2/10, n/30

DATE		DESCRIPTION	POST. REF.	DEBIT	CREDIT	BALANCE

NAME Brian's Lamp Manufacturing
ADDRESS 1339 River Road
Yardley, PA 19067

TERMS: 2/10, n/30

DATE		DESCRIPTION	POST. REF.	DEBIT	CREDIT	BALANCE
20	XX					
May	1	Balance	✓			7 9 6 2 00

NAME Kennedy Welding Supply
ADDRESS 548 Perry Street
Trenton, NJ 08648

TERMS: 2/10, n/30

DATE		DESCRIPTION	POST. REF.	DEBIT	CREDIT	BALANCE

Practice Set (continued)

Name ______________________

Brennan Lighting

Schedule of Accounts Payable

May 31, 20XX

CREDITOR	BALANCE

See the self-check key at the back of this workbook.

Brennan Lighting

Schedule of Accounts Receivable

May 31, 20XX

CUSTOMER	BALANCE

See the self-check key at the back of this workbook.

Practice Set (continued)

Brennan Lighting

Worksheet

Month Ended May 31, 20XX

	ACCT. NO.	ACCOUNT NAME	TRIAL BALANCE		ADJUSTMENTS	
			DEBIT	CREDIT	DEBIT	CREDIT
1	101	Cash				
2	102	Petty Cash				
3	112	Accounts Receivable				
4	113	Allow. for Uncoll. Accts.				
5	114	Merchandise Inventory				
6	115	Supplies				
7	116	Prepaid Insurance				
8	121	Store Equipment				
9	122	Accum. Depreciation —				
10		Store Equipment				
11	123	Office Equipment				
12	124	Accum. Depreciation —				
13		Office Equipment				
14	201	Notes Payable				
15	202	Accounts Payable				
16	221	Employee Inc. Tax Payable				
17	222	Social Security Tax Payable				
18	223	Medicare Tax Payable				
19	224	Fed. Unempl. Tax Payable				
20	225	State Unempl. Tax Payable				
21	231	Sales Tax Payable				
22	301	Tricia Brennan, Capital				
23	302	Tricia Brennan, Withdrawals				
24	399	Income Summary				
25	401	Sales				
26	402	Sales Ret. & Allow.				
27	403	Sales Discount				
28	491	Interest Income				
29	501	Merchandise Purchases				
30	502	Freight In				
31	503	Purchases Ret. & Allow.				
32	504	Purchases Discount				
33		Carried Forward				

Note: When you reach the last line of this form, add the amounts in each column and bring the totals forward to the next page.

Practice Set (continued)

Name ______________________________

ADJUSTED TRIAL BALANCE		INCOME STATEMENT		BALANCE SHEET	
DEBIT	CREDIT	DEBIT	CREDIT	DEBIT	CREDIT

Practice Set (continued)

Brennan Lighting

Worksheet

Month Ended May 31, 20XX

ACCT. NO.	ACCOUNT NAME	TRIAL BALANCE		ADJUSTMENTS	
		DEBIT	CREDIT	DEBIT	CREDIT
	Brought Forward				
511	Advertising Expense				
512	Telephone Expense				
513	Depr. Exp. — Store Equip.				
514	Depr. Exp. — Office Equip.				
516	Payroll Taxes Expense				
517	Rent Expense				
518	Supplies Expense				
519	Utilities Expense				
520	Salaries Expense				
521	Uncoll. Accts. Expense				
522	Insurance Expense				
536	Miscellaneous Expense				
	Totals				
	Net Income				

See the self-check key at the back of this workbook.

Practice Set (continued)

Name ______________________________

ADJUSTED TRIAL BALANCE		INCOME STATEMENT		BALANCE SHEET	
DEBIT	CREDIT	DEBIT	CREDIT	DEBIT	CREDIT

Practice Set (continued)

Brennan Lighting

Income Statement

Month Ended May 31, 20XX

Operating Revenue			
Sales			
Less: Sales Returns and Allowances			
Sales Discount			
Net Sales			
Cost of Goods Sold			
Merchandise Inventory, May 1			
Merchandise Purchases			
Freight In			
Delivered Cost of Purchases			
Less: Purchases Returns and Allowances			
Purchases Discount			
Net Delivered Cost of Purchases			
Total Merchandise Available for Sale			
Less: Merchandise Inventory, May 31			
Cost of Goods Sold			
Gross Profit on Sales			
Operating Expenses			
Advertising Expense			
Telephone Expense			
Depreciation Expense — Store Equipment			
Depreciation Expense — Office Equipment			
Payroll Taxes Expense			
Rent Expense			
Supplies Expense			
Utilities Expense			
Salaries Expense			
Uncollectible Accounts Expense			
Insurance Expense			
Miscellaneous Expense			
Total Operating Expenses			
Net Income From Operations			
Other Income			
Interest Income			
Net Income for the Month			

See the self-check key at the back of this workbook.

Name ______________________

Brennan Lighting

Statement of Owner's Equity

Month Ended May 31, 20XX

Tricia Brennan, Capital, May 1		
Net Income		
Less Withdrawals		
Net Increase in Owner's Equity		
Tricia Brennan, Capital, May 31		

See the self-check key at the back of this workbook.

Practice Set (continued)

Brennan Lighting

Balance Sheet

May 31, 20XX

Assets		
Current Assets		
Cash		
Petty Cash		
Accounts Receivable		
Less: Allowance for Uncollectible Accounts		
Merchandise Inventory		
Supplies		
Prepaid Insurance		
Total Current Assets		
Plant and Equipment		
Store Equipment		
Less: Accumulated Depreciation		
Office Equipment		
Less: Accumulated Depreciation		
Total Plant and Equipment		
Total Assets		
Liabilities and Owners Equity		
Current Liabilities		
Notes Payable		
Accounts Payable		
Employee Income Tax Payable		
Social Security Tax Payable		
Medicare Tax Payable		
Federal Unemployment Tax Payable		
State Unemployment Tax Payable		
Sales Tax Payable		
Total Current Liabilities		
Owner's Equity		
Tricia Brennan, Capital		
Total Liabilities and Owner's Equity		

See the self-check key at the back of this workbook.

Name ____________________

Brennan Lighting

Postclosing Trial Balance

May 31, 20XX

ACCT. NO.	ACCOUNT NAME	DEBIT	CREDIT

See the self-check key at the back of this workbook.

Extra Form

Extra Form

Name ______________________________

GENERAL JOURNAL

PAGE ________

DATE		DESCRIPTION	POST. REF.	DEBIT	CREDIT

Extra Form

NO. ______

DATE		DESCRIPTION	POST REF.	DEBIT	CREDIT	BALANCE	
						DEBIT	CREDIT

NO. ______

DATE		DESCRIPTION	POST REF.	DEBIT	CREDIT	BALANCE	
						DEBIT	CREDIT

NO. ______

DATE		DESCRIPTION	POST REF.	DEBIT	CREDIT	BALANCE	
						DEBIT	CREDIT

NO. ______

DATE		DESCRIPTION	POST REF.	DEBIT	CREDIT	BALANCE	
						DEBIT	CREDIT

Extra Form

Name ____________________

CASH RECEIPTS JOURNAL for Month of ____________________ 20 ______ PAGE ______

DATE	EXPLANATION	ACCOUNTS RECEIVABLE		SALES TAX PAYABLE CREDIT	SALES CREDIT	OTHER ACCOUNTS CREDIT			SALES DISCOUNT DEBIT	CASH DEBIT
		✓	CREDIT			ACCOUNT NAME	POST REF.	AMOUNT		

Extra Form

CASH PAYMENTS JOURNAL for Month of ____________ 20 ____ PAGE ____

DATE	CHECK NO.	EXPLANATION	ACCOUNTS PAYABLE		MERCHANDISE PURCHASES DEBIT	OTHER ACCOUNTS DEBIT			PUCHASES DISCOUNT CREDIT	CASH CREDIT
			✓	DEBIT		ACCOUNT NAME	POST REF.	AMOUNT		

Extra Form

Name ____________________

PURCHASES JOURNAL for Month of ____________________ 20 ____ PAGE ____

DATE		CREDITOR'S ACCOUNT CREDITED	POST REF.	INVOICE NUMBER	INV. DATE	TERMS	ACCOUNTS PAYABLE CREDIT	MERCH. PURCHASES DEBIT	FREIGHT IN DEBIT

PURCHASES JOURNAL for Month of ____________________ 20 ____ PAGE ____

DATE		CREDITOR'S ACCOUNT CREDITED	POST REF.	INVOICE NUMBER	INV. DATE	TERMS	ACCOUNTS PAYABLE CREDIT	MERCH. PURCHASES DEBIT	FREIGHT IN DEBIT

Extra Form

SALES JOURNAL for Month of ____________ 20 ____ PAGE ____

DATE		INV. NO.	CUSTOMER'S NAME	ACCOUNTS RECEIVABLE		SALES TAX PAYABLE CREDIT	SALES CREDIT
				✓	DEBIT		

SALES JOURNAL for Month of ____________ 20 ____ PAGE ____

DATE		INV. NO.	CUSTOMER'S NAME	ACCOUNTS RECEIVABLE		SALES TAX PAYABLE CREDIT	SALES CREDIT
				✓	DEBIT		

Extra Form

Name ______________________

PAYROLL REGISTER

WEEK BEGINNING ______________ 20 ____ AND ENDING ______________ 20 ____ PAID ______________ 20 ____

EMP. NO.	NAME	WITH. ALLOW.	MARITAL STATUS	HOURS WORKED		REG. HRLY. RATE	OVER-TIME RATE	EARNINGS			DEDUCTIONS				NET PAY	
				REG.	OVER-TIME			REGULAR	OT.	TOTAL	INCOME TAX	SOC. SEC.	MEDI-CARE	TOTAL	AMOUNT	CK. NO.

Extra Form

	ACCT. NO.	ACCOUNT NAME	TRIAL BALANCE		ADJUSTMENTS	
			DEBIT	CREDIT	DEBIT	CREDIT
1						
2						
3						
4						
5						
6						
7						
8						
9						
10						
11						
12						
13						
14						
15						
16						
17						
18						
19						
20						
21						
22						
23						
24						
25						
26						
27						
28						
29						
30						
31						
32						
33						

Name ______________________________

ADJUSTED TRIAL BALANCE		INCOME STATEMENT		BALANCE SHEET		
DEBIT	CREDIT	DEBIT	CREDIT	DEBIT	CREDIT	
						1
						2
						3
						4
						5
						6
						7
						8
						9
						10
						11
						12
						13
						14
						15
						16
						17
						18
						19
						20
						21
						22
						23
						24
						25
						26
						27
						28
						29
						30
						31
						32
						33

SELF-CHECKS FOR PROBLEMS, PROJECTS, AND PRACTICE SET

Problem 1-1. Total assets, $50,000.

Problem 1-2. Transaction C, Furniture and Accounts Payable. Transaction F, Accounts Payable and Cash.

Problem 1-3. Final totals, $6,900 + $4,500 + $22,000 = $5,400 + $28,000.

Problem 1-4. Final totals, $9,500 + $400 + $4,600 = $2,100 + $12,400.

Problem 2-1. Final totals: total assets, $18,850; liabilities, $3,500; owner's equity, $15,350. Net income, $1,350.

Problem 2-2. Final totals: total assets, $50,300; liabilities, $20,100; owner's equity, $30,200. Net loss, $1,800.

Problem 2-3. Final totals: total assets, $67,100; liabilities, $36,000; owner's equity, $31,100. Net income, $1,100.

Problem 2-4. Net income, $7,000. Total assets, $46,000.

Problem 3-1. Final totals: total assets, $145,500; liabilities, $15,500; owner's equity, $130,000. Account balances: Cash, $8,000 debit; Office Equipment, $8,000 debit; Testing Equipment $15,500 debit; Buildings, $68,000 debit; Land, $46,000 debit; Accounts Payable, $15,500 credit; Alice Russo, Capital, $130,000 credit.

Problem 3-2. Final totals: total assets, $106,000; liabilities, $36,000; owner's equity, $70,000. Account balances; Cash, $18,500 debit; Office Equipment, $6,500 debit; Towing Equipment, $33,000 debit; Building, $34,000 debit; Land, $14,000 debit; Loans Payable, $31,000 credit; Accounts Payable, $5,000 credit; Thomas Rubin, Capital, $70,000 credit.

Problem 4-1. Net income, $1,120. Increase in owner's equity, $520.

Problem 4-2. Net income, $1,000. Increase in owner's equity, $600.

Problem 5-1. Trial balance totals, $113,900.

Problem 5-2. Trial balance totals, $42,300.

Problem 5-3. Trial balance totals, $54,200.

Problem 5-4. Trial balance totals, $65,442.

Problem 5-5. Trial balance totals, $10,000.

Problem 6-1. Net income, $1,752. Capital on January 31, $22,512. Total assets, $32,112.

Problem 6-2. Net income, $1,000. Capital on April 30, $38,800. Total assets, $50,200.

Project 1. Trial balance totals, $53,200. Net income, $997. Capital on December 31, $47,297. Total assets, $51,247.

Problem 7-1. Compare the format of your journal entries with those shown in Chapter 7 of the text. Make sure that you recorded equal debits and credits in each entry. The July 12 entry should include a debit to Accounts Receivable. The July 21 entry should include a credit to Accounts Receivable. The first entry on July 25 should include a debit to Accounts Payable.

Problem 7-2. The August 7 entry should include credits to Cash and Accounts Payable. The August 10 entry should include credits to Truck Delivery Fees and Messenger Service Fees.

Problem 8-1. Trial balance totals, $31,820.

Problem 8-2. Trial balance totals, $39,555.

Problem 9-1. Completed worksheet: Income Statement Debit column total, $2,810; Balance Sheet Credit column total, $30,420. Net loss, $1,410; capital on July 31, $18,940; total assets, $28,610.

Problem 9-2. Completed worksheet: Income Statement Credit column total, $5,880; Balance Sheet Debit column total, $35,859. Net income, $2,184; capital on August 31, $30,384; total assets, $34,859.

Problem 9-3. Completed worksheet: Trial Balance Debit column total, $16,950; Income Statement Credit column, $1,420; Balance Sheet Debit column total, $16,080. Net income, $550; capital on April 30, $15,110; total assets, $15,630.

Problem 10-1. Your general journal should contain four closing entries. The third entry should transfer a net loss of $1,410 to the capital account. Postclosing trial balance totals, $28,610.

Problem 10-2. Your general journal should contain four closing entries. The third entry should transfer a net income of $2,184 to the capital account. Postclosing trial balance totals, $34,859.

Project 2. Completed worksheet: Trial Balance column totals, $39,225; Income Statement Credit column total, $10,250; Balance Sheet Debit column total, $34,256. Net income, $5,281; capital on March 31, $32,181; total assets, $33,556. Postclosing trial balance totals, $33,556.

Problem 11-1.
a. Total sales slip amount, $62.83.
b. Sales tax, $2.06.

Problem 11-2.
a. Amount of discount, $3.95.
b. Amount of payment, $332.71.
c. Last day to deduct discount, August 1.

Problem 11-3. Discount, $55.93; Amount of payment, $2,880.40.

Problem 11-4. 1. a. Last day for payment, May 8.
e. Last day to deduct discount, November 10.
2. a. Amount of payment, $650.
b. Amount of payment, $1,800.

Problem 12-1. Corrected total in Invoice 945, $832.

Problem 12-2. a. Amount of discount, $9.82.
b. Amount of payment, $823.68.

Problem 13-1. Accounts Payable balance, $3,000. Trial balance totals, $23,576.

Problem 14-1. Accounts Receivable balance, $1,123.50. Trial balance totals, $36,716.05.

Problem 15-1. Sales journal: Accounts Receivable Debit column total, $1,501.50.

Problem 15-2. Trial balance totals, $13,911.26.

Problem 16-1. Purchases journal: Accounts Payable Credit column total, $4,638.60.

Problem 16-2. Trial balance totals, $16,996.63.

Problem 17-1. Cash receipts journal: Cash Debit column total, $10,508.25. Trial balance totals, $24,618.14.

Problem 17-2. Cash receipts journal: Cash Debit column total, $16,207.78. Trial balance totals, $28,578.48

Problem 18-1. Cash payments journal: Cash Credit column total, $4,007.45.

Problem 18-2. Cash payments journal: Cash Credit column total, $9,806.75. Trial balance totals, $48,026.48.

Problem 19-1. August 30 account balance for Reynolds Hardware Store, $625.00

Problem 19-2. Cash receipts journal: Cash Debit column total, $6,647.72. Sales journal: Accounts Receivable Debit column total, $1,664.25. Total of schedule of accounts receivable, $908.25. February 28 account balance for Chew's Market, $157.50

Problem 20-1. October 28 account balance for Crafter Manufacturing Company, $1,288.30.

Problem 20-2. Cash payments journal: Cash Credit column total, $4,350.65. Purchases journal: Accounts Payable Credit column total, $3,522.00. Total of schedule of accounts payable, $2,561.00

Project 3

Cash receipts journal column totals: Accounts Receivable Credit, $3,446.10; Sales Tax Payable Credit, $442.04; Sales Credit, $8,840.60; Other Accounts Credit, $120.00; Sales Discount Debit, $48.84; and Cash Debit, $12,799.90.

Cash payments journal column totals: Accounts Payable Debit, $2,245.00; Merchandise Purchases Debit, $450.00; Other Accounts Debit, $9,395.20; Purchase Discount Credit, $30.40; and Cash Credit, $12,059.80.

Sales journal column totals: Accounts Receivable Debit, $8,176.14; Sales Tax Payable Credit, $389.34; and Sales Credit, $7,786.80.

Purchases journal column totals: Accounts Payable Credit, $6,782.00; Merchandise Purchases Debit, $6,575.00 and Freight In Debit, $207.00

Total of schedule of accounts receivable, $4,625.04.

Total of schedule of accounts payable, $4,387.00

Trial Balance totals, $66,021.18.

Problem 21-1. Trial Balance column totals, $81,210; Adjustments column totals, $41,970; Adjusted Trial Balance column totals, $103,005.

Problem 21-2. Trial Balance column totals, $82,785; Adjustments column totals, $37,025; Adjusted Trial Balance column totals, $100,950.

Problem 22-1. Net income $10,480. Capital as of March 31, $57,100. Total assets, $59,800.

Problem 22-2. Net income $2,015. Capital as of December 31, $44,140. Total assets, $45,900.

Problem 22-3. Adjustments column totals, $19,320; Adjusted Trial Balance column totals, $58,990. Net income, $3,540.

Problem 23-1. The third closing entry should transfer a net income of $10,480 to the capital account.

Problem 23-2. The third closing entry should transfer a net income of $2,015 to the capital account. Postclosing trial balance totals, $47,665.

Project 4

Worksheet column totals: Trial Balance, $66,021.18; Adjustments, $35,347.50; Adjusted Trial Balance, $83,206.18; Income Statement, $33,807.80; Balance Sheet, $52,240.14.

Closing entries: The third closing entry should transfer a net income of $2,841.76 to the capital account.

Income statement: net income, $2,841.76

Statement of owner's equity: capital as of February 28, $45,841.76

Balance sheet: total assets, $51,055.14.

Postclosing trial balance totals: $51,240.14.

Problem 24-1. Deposit slip total, $357.28

Problem 24-2. Check stub balance, $3,482.58.

Problem 24-3. Adjusted bank balance and checkbook balance, $1,509.43.

Problem 24-4. Adjusted bank balance and checkbook balance, $9,933.12

Problem 25-1. Total cash on hand, $28.28. Amount requested for replenishment, $46.72.

Problem 25-2. Cash receipts journal column totals: Sales Tax Payable Credit, $102.95; Sales Credit, $2,058.85; Cash Short or (Over) Debit, $1.97; Cash Debit, $2,159.83.

Problem 26-1. Gross Earnings, $380; net pay, $293.43.

Problem 26-2. Payroll register column totals: Regular Earnings, $2,348; Overtime Earnings, $441.15; Total Earnings, $2,789.15; Income Tax, $161; and Net Pay, $2,414.78.

Problem 26-3. Debit to Salaries and Wages Expense, $1,976.80. Debit to Payroll Taxes Expense, $259.94.

Problem 26-4. No check answer.

Problem 27-1. Combined journal column totals: Cash Debit, $10,139.98; Cash Credit, $7,186.33; Accounts Receivable Debit, $3,217; Accounts Receivable Credit, $2,871; Accounts Payable Debit, $3,348; Accounts Payable Credit, $5,498; Merchandise Purchases Debit, $5,498; Sales Credit, $10,543.40; Other Accounts Debit, $6,296.54; Other Accounts Credit, $2,400.79; Proof of combined journal totals, $28,499.52.

Practice Set

Sales journal column totals: Accounts Receivable Debit, $22,651.84; Sales Tax Payable Credit, $1,282.18; Sales Credit, $21,369.66.

Purchases journal column totals: Accounts Payable Credit, $31,528.88; Merchandise Purchases Debit, $30,808.40; Freight In Debit, $720.48.

Cash receipts journal column totals: Accounts Receivable Credit, $8,553.14; Sales Tax Payable Credit, $3,272.01; Sales Credit, $54,533.59; Other Accounts Credit, $3,775; Sales Discount Debit, $56.41; Cash Debit, $70,077.33.

Cash payments journal column totals: Accounts Payable Debit $26,400.39; Merchandise Purchases Debit, $1,967.24; Other Accounts Debit, $33,483.81; Purchases Discount Credit $471.74; Cash Credit, $61,379.70.

Total of schedule of accounts payable, $4,990.15.

Total of schedule of accounts receivable, $15,936.64.

Worksheet totals: Trial Balance columns, $260,828.80; Adjustments columns, $96,760.42; Adjusted Trial Balance columns, $300,334.66; Income Statement Debit column (before net income), $112,866.41; Income Statement Credit column, $116,310.19. Balance Sheet Debit column, $187,468.25; Balance Sheet Credit column (before net income), $184,024.47.

Income statement: net income, $3,443.78.

Statement of owner's equity: Capital, May 31, $142,399.33.

Balance sheet: total assets, $163,959.25.

Postclosing trial balance totals, $184,468.25.